D1237911

RED WAGONS
AND
WHITE CANVAS

For Betsy — asking
Thanks for asking
me to River Oaks Baptist
School. I enjoyed it —
Mary Surasich 11/3/88

RED WAGONS AND WHITE CANVAS

A
STORY
OF THE
MOLLIE
BAILEY
CIRCUS

Marj Gurasich

EAKIN PRESS   Austin, Texas

In memory of
Mother and Dad
who always believed

Contents

Acknowledgments

No book is ever written without the aid and encouragement of family, friends, and "helpful others." Accordingly, I wish to express my thanks to those who helped so very much in putting *Red Wagons and White Canvas* together.

Particular thanks goes to my special friends — librarians. Without exception, they exhibited untiring patience and expertise in assisting me with my research. Each library I visited had something different to offer, and I would like to thank them all: Texas Room, Houston Public Library; Clayton Genealogical Library, Houston, Texas; George Memorial Library, Richmond, Texas; Knox Memorial Library, Wallis, Texas; Eugene C. Barker Texas History Center, University of Texas, Austin, Texas; Harry Ransom Humanities Research Center, Theater Arts Library, UT, Austin, Texas.

Of immense value was information gleaned from the files of the Hertzberg Circus Collection, San Antonio Public Library, San Antonio, Texas, with the aid of librarian Betty Claire King. Research librarian Bill McCarthy spent many hours assisting me in locating circus pictures at the Research Library, Circus World Museum, Baraboo, Wisconsin. Both libraries are treasure troves of circus lore.

My husband, Stephen, deserves my heartfelt appreciation for his patience and understanding of how important this project was to me. And our merger-marriage accumulation of ten children made a marvelous support

vii

group. Thanks to one and all, especially daughters Wendy and Barbara, my best critics and friends.

A final thanks to my publisher, Ed Eakin, without whom this story would still be tucked in a manuscript box on a shelf, and to the future readers of *Red Wagons and White Canvas*. They are the ones, after all, who breathe life into a book and make it, for a little while, part of themselves.

Preface

Mollie Bailey, affectionately known by several generations of Texans as Aunt Mollie, ran the Mollie A. Bailey Show, "A Texas Show for Texas People," from around 1870 until her death in 1918.

Mollie eloped with James A. (Gus) Bailey when she was fourteen, in 1858. Gus, cornet player in his father's circus band, was no relation to the Bailey of Barnum and Bailey Circus. When Mollie ran away from her family's plantation in Alabama, she left behind an unforgiving father, William Kirkland, and a broken-hearted mother, Mary Arline Kirkland. Her father never spoke to her again or acknowledged her as his daughter. Before she and her new husband left, Mollie "borrowed" horses and a wagon from the plantation. She felt she deserved them.

The Baileys traveled throughout the South, entertaining people everywhere they went. Before and after the War Between the States, they ran the Bailey Family Troupe, the Bailey Concert Company, a showboat on the Mississippi River and, finally, the circus.

Red Wagons and White Canvas portrays the Mollie Bailey Show as it probably was in 1890. Outside of Mollie and her family, the characters are fictitious.

1

The Circus Comes to Huntsville

1890

Jeremiah glanced both ways, then shinnied under the bottom edge of canvas. He was almost inside when something caught and held his bare ankle. He twisted and wriggled, but he couldn't get free. He closed his eyes. If he didn't look, maybe whatever held him would go away. But he felt himself being pulled back under the tent until warm sunshine fell on his face.

"Well, young man, just what do you think you're doin'?"

The voice was a woman's, a soft Southern voice with an edge of anger in it. But, Jeremiah thought, it didn't sound *too* angry. He tested his feelings by opening one eye.

"Come, come, answer me. What were you doin' under the tent?"

The owner of the voice was standing over him, glowering down at him. He shivered but told himself he wasn't afraid.

"I . . . ah . . . I wanted to see the circus, ma'am," he said, surprised at how small and frightened his voice sounded. "And I didn't have the quarter for a ticket."

1

"Well, we have ways to deal with the likes of you," the woman said. "Cy," she called, "come here and get this thief. He tried to steal himself into the show. What did we do with the last one who did that?"

Jeremiah shuddered. Cy was a hulk of a man, and he looked at Jeremiah and shook his head.

"Oy, it were bad, what happened to that youngun. Beat him, we did, till he had to be carried home, like a babe."

Jeremiah felt the blood drain from his face. He scrambled to his feet and stood, scrunching his bare toes into the warm dust.

"Please, ma'am, I'm awful sorry I tried to sneak in. I did so want to see the elephant, Bolivar. I heard tell he's ever so smart. Please, don't beat me."

He could feel the tears behind his eyes pushing to get free. But he wouldn't let them, no matter what these circus people did to him. He squeezed his eyes tightly shut and waited for his punishment.

It was a moment before he heard the laughter. The woman and man were *laughing!* Whatever did they think was funny about beating a poor defenseless boy?

"Open your eyes, son," the woman said, putting a hand softly on his shoulder. "We just wanted to give you a bit of a scare. You've had your punishment. Now tell me your name and where you live hereabouts."

Jeremiah let out his breath in a sigh of relief and opened his eyes again. The woman was smiling at him with dark gypsy eyes that crinkled at the corners. Cy was walking away, still laughing.

"My name is Jeremiah Colquitt, ma'am, and I live down Mill Road, just past the bridge," he said, brushing the dust from his shirt and pants and staring up at the woman. She wasn't stooped and tired-looking like Ma, and she wore her black hair piled high on her head. Her dress was of some dark stiff material and smelled vaguely of cedar and lavender. "I'm mighty glad you're not mad at me anymore," he added with a shy smile. He liked the way she looked at him, as though he was worth listening to. It made him feel good inside. He finger-combed his white-blond hair off his forehead.

"Tarnation, Jeremiah, I never was mad at you. Just having a little fun to teach you a lesson. It's not a good idea to take things that don't belong to you, even if it's just a look at the circus," she said. "Why didn't you come this morning and water the elephant? You could have earned yourself a ticket."

"I was here, ma'am. Before the sun came up, I was sitting on the fence waiting for the circus wagons to come by. After they passed I ran to the lot, but they took all the big fellers first and didn't ever get to me. I couldn't ask Ma. She has these ends she keeps trying to make meet, but they never do. I knew she wouldn't have the money for a circus ticket. I . . . I'm really sorry I tried to sneak in."

"Yes, son, I know all about tryin' to make ends meet." The dark eyes smiled at him in understanding. "Come on, you can get in the right way, through the entrance flap. You've already missed the tournament. That's the grand entrance parade when everyone in the circus struts around the ring, showin' off. But Bolivar is about to start his routine. Hear the band? That's his tune they're playin'."

"Oh, thank you . . ." Jeremiah was at a loss for words.

"My name is Mollie Bailey, son. This is my circus and everyone calls me Aunt Mollie."

"Thank you, er . . . ah . . . Aunt Mollie."

"Now off with you. Hustle on in. You're missin' the show."

Jeremiah ran to the front of the big tent and, with a feeling of wonder, stepped into another world: the world of the *circus!*

"La-deez and gentlemen! And children of all ages! May I have your atten-shun!"

3

The ringmaster was dressed in a bright red waist-coat, and his white breeches were tucked into knee-high shiny black boots. He wore a black top hat and carried a riding crop. Jeremiah thought he had never seen such a handsome man. His voice boomed through the tent, and an expectant hush fell over the crowd.

"The Bailey Circus is proud to present its *star attraction* . . . Bolivar, the performing elephant from darkest *Africa!*"

As the ringmaster went on about Bolivar, Jeremiah gazed around him. Rows and rows of blue-painted benches, filled with laughing, noisy folks, surrounded the outer edges of the big tent. The top row was just beneath the tent's canvas roof. At the far end of the tent a stage held the circus band dressed in bright red coats with brass buttons. In the center of the tent was a huge ring made of piled-up dirt.

Looking overhead, Jeremiah saw wires and ropes hanging from the ceiling like spider webs. A swing lazily moved so high above his head it made him dizzy.

He was more excited than he had ever been in his whole life. And he hadn't seen any of the circus yet!

He took a deep breath of pure happiness. His nose picked up an earth and animal smell, raw on the air. He liked it. It was the circus.

The ringmaster's voice cut through Jeremiah's thoughts. He got louder and louder as he described the show about to go on.

"Bolivar will astound and delight you as he performs difficult and dangerous tricks for your pleasure. . . . *Here he is, folks! Bo..li..varrrrr!*"

With a flourish of his top hat and a deep bow, the ringmaster backed out of the ring. Jeremiah's eyes turned to the elephant.

The animal looked even bigger than he had in the early morning light on the circus lot. Jeremiah marveled at his thick, wrinkled skin. It hung in great, gray folds from his body as though part of his stuffing had fallen out. Bolivar's giant-sized ears flapped as he lumbered along. They had been painted with red, yellow, and purple flowers, and on top of his huge head he wore a pad embroidered in glistening silver threads. The most beautiful girl Jeremiah had ever seen sat on the pad and waved to the audience. She had golden hair and wore a filmy pink dress bright with spangles.

Jeremiah laughed when he saw that the elephant's tail had purple and silver ribbons braided around it. The ends of the ribbons fluttered in the air as he slowly plodded around the ring.

For the next few minutes Jeremiah sat as still as stone, entranced by the wonders of Bolivar.

First the elephant bent his back knees and lowered his mighty head. The golden-haired girl slid down his trunk to the ground. Jeremiah thought her as graceful as a butterfly, and as beautiful. She and the elephant took deep bows as the crowd applauded. The girl then lay down between the elephant's front legs, and the huge beast lowered himself over her body.

Jeremiah's heart stood still. Surely Bolivar would crush the life out of her. All noise within the tent stopped. Jeremiah wanted to close his eyes as he always did when he was frightened, but his curiosity wouldn't let him.

Bolivar hoisted himself up again and the girl jumped to her feet and raised her arms to the crowd. Again, cheers and applause.

Jeremiah let out his breath and sighed. What a wonderful place the circus was! How grand to perform for people and make them love you as everyone there loved the golden girl and her elephant.

Bolivar balanced on one hind foot and stood straight up. Next, he danced in time to the band's waltzing tune. He then took a deep bow for the applause he deserved. The girl climbed back on top of his head and patted him on the ear. "Good job, Bolivar," she must have said, thought Jeremiah.

As the elephant left the ring, Jeremiah felt that the

best of the circus must be over. But in came the clowns, and he had to laugh aloud. Each one wore a baggy clown suit, a pointed cap, and special clown-face makeup. No two were alike.

One clown, dressed in white with huge red polka dots, also had red polka dots painted on top of his bald head. He carried a small pink pig that had a blue baby bonnet on his head. When the piglet squealed, the clown pulled a large baby bottle out of his pocket. The little pig took the nipple eagerly, and the two wandered around the ring to the delight of Jeremiah and all the other spectators.

The rest of the clowns chased one another around, slapping at each other, falling down and pretending to be in great pain. By the time they all trooped out of the ring, Jeremiah's jaws hurt from laughing so hard.

As he recovered from his laughter, Jeremiah's nose began to twitch. A heavenly smell had reached it — popcorn. Suddenly, his stomach churned with hunger pangs. He was thirsty too. When he saw a man hand a pink lemonade to a small girl, Jeremiah licked his lips. He could almost taste that icy cool tartness.

But Jeremiah turned away. He had no money to buy eats or drinks. He was lucky to be there at all. He needed to remember that and be grateful.

The rest of the afternoon passed all too swiftly. He watched the slack wire performer, the jugglers, the acrobats leaping onto each other's shoulders until they were seven high. He laughed at the trained ponies and dogs as they jumped through hoops and climbed ladders. The beautiful equestrienne, on her white horse, dazzled his eyes as she rode round and round the dirt ring. When she stood on one foot with the other high in the air behind her and threw kisses at the crowd, Jeremiah felt a lump in his throat.

The last act, and the best, he thought, was the Flying Morenos, "Aerialists Supreme," who performed on the trapeze. Jeremiah sat spellbound as the family, a father, mother, two sons, and a daughter, flew back and forth through the air like a flock of wild, soaring birds. The father did not fly but hung by his knees on one swing and caught the others as they left the other swing to do daring feats in midair.

Dressed in spangled tights and brief tops, the Morenos made Jeremiah's heart thrill. Several times, he had to close his eyes; they surely must fall this time. But each time the father caught his "bird" by the wrists and they swung together until he let go and the bird returned to its nest.

The circus was a world all to itself, Jeremiah thought. What a wonderful way to live! The performers traveled all over the country, seeing sights and having fun. And there would prob'ly be no school to go to, if they were on the road all the time. How he would love circus life!

The thought crept into his head without his giving it permission. The first thing he knew, it was just there. He closed his eyes for a moment, but the thought didn't go away. It only got stronger and stronger.

Why shouldn't he join the circus and live this life of fun and travel too? Maybe he could learn to fly. . . . Ma would not have to feed him anymore or buy him clothes. He would send her all the money he earned. Then maybe she could make those ends meet after all.

Jeremiah couldn't think of a single reason not to join the circus. He was already ten years old, though Ma said he was small for his age. He could water old Bolivar as well as those big fellers could. Maybe, just maybe, he could learn to walk the tightrope or ride a horse while standing proudly on its back.

He could see his circus days stretching out before him. Such excitement overtook him that he lost his balance and toppled off the bleacher, landing beneath the seats in the dust.

7

He shook the dirt out of his eyes and looked around. He was nearly on the same spot where Aunt Mollie had discovered him just a few hours ago. But Jeremiah was not the same person. No, sir.

Now he belonged to the circus.

Now he belonged to the Molly Bailey Show.

2

Wagon Stowaway

Jeremiah saw the rest of the show in a daze. His mind was whirling with plans about joining the circus. He didn't dare go home. Ma would guess by the excited look on his face that he was up to something. She always knew.

As soon as the show was over, the men would start pulling the tents down. Jeremiah decided to find an empty wagon and hide in it until they reached the next town. Aunt Mollie would be glad to have another hand around the show. He would work very hard to prove that he was worthy of being part of her circus.

When the show ended, the tent emptied fast. Everyone wanted to visit the menagerie and see all the wild animals in their cages before it was time to go home. Jeremiah climbed down from his seat and mingled with the crowd. He wished he had something to eat. He hadn't eaten all day.

He found a spot where he could watch the men tear down the tents, but not be seen by them. The boss man was shouting orders.

In a short time the workmen had removed the bleachers from the tent and stacked them into one of the red wooden wagons. They knocked down the stage where the band had sat and packed it away. Then Jeremiah watched with amazement as men and boys struggled with poles, ropes, and canvas.

"Lower away!" shouted the crew boss. The tent dropped to the ground with a whoosh and a sigh. The bare center pole followed it to the ground. The men rushed in to fold and cart away the canvas while others hauled off the long pole. Soon all that was left of the circus was sawdust blowing in the wind and peanut shells crunching underfoot.

It was beginning to get dark. Someone lit torches for light as the men packed up the gold-trimmed red wagons. The sound of stakes, chains, and poles being loaded echoed around the bare lot. When Jeremiah saw boys hitching horses to the wagons, he knew it was almost time for the circus to leave. He would have to find a hiding place quickly.

He ran alongside the wagons, which had been formed into a line before hitching up the horses. When he got nearly to the front, he heard a shout.

"Hey, who's that?"

It sounded like Cy, the man he had met earlier that morning. Jeremiah shuddered at the thought of how big and scary he was. Ducking his head, he grabbed the handrail of the nearest wagon and pulled himself up the steps. Inside he leaned against the door and took a deep breath.

He looked around and ducked for cover under a narrow bed, barely squeezing beneath it. He lay on the cool floor, panting, and his eyes were closed. With luck, Cy would not look further for him.

His eyes quickly opened. Something was different.

The wagon was moving!

He must have kept his eyes closed so long that he

10

had fallen asleep. How long had he slept? Where were they by now?

Then he stiffened. He heard a voice. He strained his ears to hear. If it was Cy . . . he shuddered. No, it was a woman's voice. He lifted the heavy bed covering which hung to the floor and dared a peek.

It was Aunt Mollie!

Jeremiah dropped the cover and took a deep breath. He would just stay hidden until tomorrow. Then she couldn't send him home. She'd welcome another hand around the circus.

"Ka---choo!"

The deep breath he had taken had been filled with dust. Oh, gol, now he had done it. His eyes were closed tight, but he could feel fresh air on his face. Someone had lifted the quilt and was looking under the bed.

For the second time that day, something grabbed his ankle. He felt himself being pulled out of his hiding place. This time he knew who it was.

"You!" Aunt Mollie's voice penetrated his fear. "What in tarnation are you doin' here, boy? Jeremy, was it?"

"Jeremiah, ma'am," his voice answered with a squeak at the end. He carefully opened his eyes.

Under the soft candlelight in the wagon, Aunt Mollie looked younger and prettier. Her shiny black hair hung loose down her back, almost to her waist. She wore a soft, long garment tied at the waist. In her hand she held a silver hairbrush that glinted softly in the flickering light.

"Well, Jeremiah, now that you've interrupted my hair brushin', what have you to say for yourself?"

The words would not come out of his dry mouth. He stammered a moment and then croaked, "I've come along to join the circus, ma'am . . . Aunt Mollie. It's all right if I join up, ain't it?"

"Let's talk about it, Jeremiah. Why do you want to join the circus?"

"Oh, ma'am, today was so wonderful and I want to be a part of it all and learn to perform and get applause and —"

"Whoa! Slow down! You've got the cart before the horse. Before you can do any of that, there's something important you didn't mention," Aunt Mollie said. She began to brush her hair in long, rhythmic strokes.

"Wha . . . What is that, ma'am?"

"Let's talk about how your folks feel about you runnin' off with the circus."

"Oh."

"What did your ma say when you told her you were goin' after all that applause?"

"Nothin', ma'am. Ma don't know it yet. I ain't never gone home after the show today. But she won't mind, honest she won't."

"Well, Jeremiah, I can see you're real serious about this circus life. So I'll tell you what. As soon as your ma says it's all right, you can come ahead. We can find plenty of work for a boy like you. Tell me, does your ma have that white-blond hair like yours? Tarnation, it looks just like cotton, it does."

Jeremiah swallowed hard. He didn't know what to say. If he had to go back and ask Ma . . . well, he knew she'd say no and that would be the end of his circus life.

"No'm," he finally got out. "Her hair is sorta brownlike. No one in my family has hair this dumb color. Whoever heard of white hair on a boy?"

He meant to say more, to tell her that Pa had died a year ago and that Ma tried to meet those ends with four growing kids to feed. That his older brothers, Joe and Will, could earn a little now and then to help out. And that his baby sister was a comfort to Ma. They'd be better off without him. Just one more mouth. They prob'ly wouldn't even miss him. But he never got it out.

Instead, he fainted.

3

Cotton Bailey

When he opened his eyes, Jeremiah realized two things. First, the wagon was no longer moving. Second, he was now on the bed, instead of under it. Feeling something cold and wet on his forehead, he reached up to see what it was.

"Leave it there, son." It was Aunt Mollie's voice. "It's just a cool cloth to help you get back to yourself. I'm wonderin' why you had that bit of a sinkin' spell. Do you have any idea?"

"No'm," Jeremiah answered, his voice small and weak.

"Well, I kind of figured you might not have eaten too much today. Is that right?"

"No'm . . . I mean yes'm, you're right. No'm, I ain't et anything today." Jeremiah felt sharp twists and turns in his stomach as soon as eating was mentioned.

"I thought so," Aunt Mollie said, nodding her head. "I just sent my son, Eugene, up to the cook's wagon to fetch you some supper. He'll be turnin' up with it pretty soon. Meantime, you just lie there and rest. Y'hear?"

"Yes'm," Jeremiah answered. He snuggled down into the quilt on Aunt Mollie's bed.

The door creaked as it opened, and a sandy-haired young man stuck his head into the wagon.

"Here's the vittles for the youngun, Maw. I gotta get back to the lead wagon. It's time we got rollin' again."

"Thank you, Gene, darlin'," Aunt Mollie said with a smile, "and thank Cook for sending this food to my young friend. Jeremiah, this is my eldest boy, Eugene. We call him Gene. Son, this is Jeremiah. Wants to join the circus."

Gene nodded in Jeremiah's direction. Jeremiah said "Howdy" in a small voice.

"If that's all you need, Maw, we'll give our horses the 'giddy'up' and head for Shiro. It's near twenty miles, so we'll have a long night's ride — 'specially after this delay. Barely make it in time for the parade."

"Yes, I know," Aunt Mollie agreed. "But, Gene, I want you to pull my wagon out of the train. I'm going to sit a spell right here in the woods."

"Wha . . . how long?"

"Till early mornin'. This boy and I have unfinished business back in Huntsville. Go on and get us out of the line. I'll hustle on into Shiro as soon as I can. You and Cy can handle the parade if I don't make it there in time."

Gene looked puzzled and glanced at Jeremiah as though he wondered what kind of spell he had cast over his mother.

Jeremiah felt heat rise from his neck to his ears and all over his face. He knew from experience that the heat meant he was turning as red as a beet, till even his scalp would show pink through his pale hair. He ducked his head so Aunt Mollie and her son wouldn't notice.

With a nod Gene left the wagon. Jeremiah could hear him talking to the horses as he moved his mother's wagon off the road. Then he yelled at the driver of the lead wagon to get going.

Jeremiah heard the rumble of the wooden wheels as

the other wagons rolled over the uneven road, away from him and Aunt Mollie.

"Don't you worry, Jeremiah — my, that's a long name for a youngun — we'll catch up to them before they reach Shiro. They can't travel very fast with Bolivar and the extra horses trailin' along on foot. We don't have a wagon big enough for that old elephant."

Jeremiah smiled. Just thinking about Bolivar made him feel happy all over. Even if he didn't have any idea what Aunt Mollie planned to do. Or what the "unfinished business" could be.

"Tarnation," Aunt Mollie said with a shake of her head. "We've been talkin' so much, you haven't eaten a bite of that food. Go after it, son, you must be starved."

Jeremiah started to eat the cold meat and cheese and tore a chunk of bread from the loaf in front of him.

"Thank you, ma'am," he managed to mumble as he chewed.

"I'm makin' you a pallet on the floor. When you finish your supper, get some sleep. We're off before dawn to head back into Huntsville, y'hear?" Aunt Mollie talked as she busied herself putting blankets and quilts on the floor for a bed for Jeremiah.

He hurried with his food and then crawled between the covers of the pallet. He didn't quite know how to say "thank you" and "goodnight" to this beautiful lady who had been so kind to him.

"Goodnight, Jeremiah," she said from her bed.

"Goodnight, Aunt Mollie. And thank you," he answered. He guessed that was the best way to say it, after all.

It was still dark when he awoke. The wagon was lumbering along the rough dirt road. He peeked out the small window in the front of the wagon. Aunt Mollie must be driving. The moon was still up there, shining brightly on the quiet woods and the horses' backs, turning them the color of silver.

16

Jeremiah concentrated to see if he recognized anything. Gol, it was Mill Road on the way home from town, and there was the bridge, just ahead. Aunt Mollie was taking him home! And he had thought she liked him and wanted him to be a part of her circus. Well, he wouldn't be in her old circus now if she begged him — on her knees, with tears in her eyes. No, sir.

He sat back down on the bed, with his knees drawn up and his head down on them. His arms were wrapped around his legs to keep them from wobbling. He couldn't believe it. Tears that hadn't escaped earlier now rolled down his cheeks as if to say, "See, we got our way, after all!"

Another peek out the window told him they were home. Ma would be mad at him for running off like he did. It didn't matter. Nothing mattered . . . now that he couldn't be in the circus.

The wagon came to a halt with a creaking sound. Jeremiah scrubbed his eyes with his sleeve. He didn't want either woman to know that he'd been crying.

"Jeremiah," called Aunt Mollie softly. "Come out, son, and go get your ma. I don't have much time."

"Yes, ma'am," Jeremiah said, his voice a low murmur.

He trudged around the house to the back door and saw his mother in the light of the kerosene lantern, mixing up hoe cakes for the younguns' breakfast. He thought wistfully of the meat and cheese he had eaten last night.

"Ma," he said, standing just outside the open door.

His mother looked up and went back to her mixing.

"Oh, it's you, Jeremiah. Where in blazes you been gone to all night? You think I have time to go lookin' for you all over the place, huh?"

"Ma, I went to the circus and the lady who owns it let me go in and watch. It was wonderful. Miz Bailey, she's the circus lady, brought me home."

"Well, get in here and wake up your brothers. They need to get out if they're goin' to look for chores to do.

17

They need to make some money if I'm to make ends meet."

Those ends again. How tired Jeremiah was of those ends that kept him from all his hopes and dreams.

"Yes'm," was all he said.

As he started up the stairs to wake his brothers, he heard Aunt Mollie's soft voice. He hid in the bend of the stairs to listen.

"Mrs. Colquitt," Aunt Mollie began. "I'm Mollie Bailey, owner of the circus that was in town yesterday. I have taken quite a shine to your boy Jeremiah, and he wants to join the circus. We came to see if you'd approve if he traveled with the show, at least till we come back this way again."

Love for Aunt Mollie overflowed Jeremiah's heart. She hadn't brought him home to leave behind. She had planned all along to take him with the circus, if Ma would just say yes. He closed his eyes as tight as he ever had. If Ma said no he would die, right there on the stairs.

He could hear the women's voices, but he was too upset to distinguish their words. Then he heard his ma say something that sounded like "it's hard enough to make ends meet, with all of them to feed. Maybe with one less mouth . . ."

She was doing it! She was saying yes! He never dreamed that those pesky ends would save him someday. Oh, gol, oh — he was going to be a circus man, after all!

For the smallest moment, a pang of sorrow touched him. It hurt just a mite that Ma would let him go so easily, just so her old ends could meet.

"Jeremiah," his mother said. "Come down off that stairway and say 'thank you' to the kind lady for takin' you in. Then get your clothes together. Miz Bailey's in a bit of a hurry."

"Yes, Ma," Jeremiah said, embarrassed to have Aunt Mollie know that he'd been listening.

Without looking at her he mumbled, "Thank ya," and stumbled out of the room.

18

It didn't take long to put his few things in a pillow sham and give a last look at his little sister Annie, who was still asleep. She was the only one he hated to leave. He touched her hair, then turned and left the room. He was ready to join Aunt Mollie and set out on their way back to the circus. The circus . . .

The truth suddenly hit him. He was going to live with Aunt Mollie and the circus people. He pinched himself to be sure he wasn't dreaming. No, the red mark and the hurt proved it. Gol.

He snatched up the bundle and raced down the stairs.

"Bye, Ma. I'll write you a letter."

"Needn't bother. If there's bad news I'll hear it fast enough."

She bent her head over the pot of cornmeal she was stirring and didn't look up again. Jeremiah glanced at Aunt Mollie, who nodded, and the two of them slipped out the door without another word.

They made good time getting to Shiro. The horses seemed to sense the need to hurry. They caught up with the snail-slow circus train about two miles outside the village. Cy took over the driving so that Aunt Mollie could ride inside the wagon, as was proper for the owner of the circus.

Already townsfolk were out to greet them. Jeremiah saw kids sitting on the fences watching them pass. Some would hurry down to the lot to try to water the elephant so they could get in.

But not *me*, he thought. *I* belong to the Mollie A. Bailey Show now. I can get pink lemonade free and watch every show and . . . .

"Jeremiah, did you hear me?" Aunt Mollie had been speaking to him and he hadn't paid any attention.

"Yes,'m?"

"I said that this is your first day with the Mollie Bailey Circus. I want you to be happy with us, Jeremiah."

"Oh yes, ma'am, I will be. I know that I will."

"One more thing," Aunt Mollie said as she started to climb down out of the wagon which had pulled into a shady spot on the edge of the circus grounds.

Jeremiah looked at Aunt Mollie, curious to know what that "thing" could be.

"Yes'm?"

"Jeremiah Colquitt is too long a name for a circus man. So from now on you're goin' to be called Cotton. For that beautiful white hair. Cotton Bailey. Yes, I like that. Cotton Bailey."

4

The New Hand
Gets Acquainted

At first Jeremiah had trouble remembering that his name was now "Cotton Bailey," but by the end of the week it seemed as though it had never been anything else. He couldn't forget, either, that Aunt Mollie had named him Cotton because of his beautiful hair. Gol, he had always hated his hair. Maybe it wasn't too bad to have white hair, especially if you were in the circus.

He had spent his first days learning circus talk. Aunt Mollie took him all around the lot, explaining as they went.

"In the circus, Cotton," she said, "a tent is called a 'top,' and the main show tent is the 'big top.' An elephant's a 'bull' and his keeper, a 'bull man.' Telling you this takes me back to when I ran away from my papa's plantation in Alabama to marry Gus Bailey and live in his pa's circus. I was only fourteen, and Papa never forgave me. But I never regretted marryin' Gus Bailey." Aunt Mollie shook her head. Cotton thought he saw a look of sadness in her face. Then she smiled at him again. "Anyway, I didn't know the right names for things either, and thought I'd never remember all of them. But I did, and you will too.

"Here's the last lesson for today: Performers are called 'kinkers' except for clowns, who are 'Joeys,' after a famous clown from the early days named Joe Grimaldi."

Cotton's head was spinning. He tried hard to remember everything. On top of it all, he also needed to learn the names of the circus people. Some of them were Aunt Mollie's children. Cy, who was a really nice guy when you got to know him, introduced him to the five Baileys.

"Aunt Mollie and Mr. Gus had nine children altogether, Cotton," Cy told him. "The first two girls died while they were still younguns. Nearly killed Aunt Mollie. Then Mattie, her next daughter, died when her baby come."

Cotton thought he could not put another new thing in his head. But Cy went on talking and he had to listen and try to remember it all.

"Minnie, Aunt Mollie's other girl, had a voice like an angel, but she never much liked circus life. She found her a man, named A. W. Mansfield he was, and they married and left.

"C'mon, boy, we can't set here jawin'. . . . I've got work to do. Let's go round up the rest of the Baileys so's you'll know 'em when yer sees 'em." Cy grabbed Cotton by the arm and propelled him along, as though it was Cotton's fault they had wasted so much of his time.

First came Gene, who had brought him the food that first night. Gene was twenty-one and Aunt Mollie's eldest son. He played tuba in the band, Cy said, and managed some of the circus business. Gene nodded at Cotton but hurried on as though he had more important things on his mind than a ten-year-old boy.

Cy called Allie down from the slack wire where he was practicing.

"Allie, say hello to Cotton. He's our new hand."

Allie acknowledged the introduction. He was eighteen, and dark, like Aunt Mollie. Cotton caught his breath when Cy said that Allie worked the tight wire, as well as the slack, and also played the alto horn.

Willie, also called W. K., was closer to Cotton's age, thirteen, and he played trombone. All the Bailey kids were musical, taking after their pa, Cy told him. Gus Bailey had played cornet and led the band until he got sick and had to stay all year at winter quarters in Blum.

"Mr. Bailey was in Hood's Texas Brigade during the war, Cotton," Cy said. "He was bandmaster and wrote a song called 'The Old Gray Mare.' He's a fine man, Mr. Bailey, and Aunt Mollie really misses him these days.

"Maybe yer noticed. We fly three flags over our big top: Old Glory, Lone Star, and the Stars and Bars. Aunt Mollie's a loyal American, but she's also a Confederate through and through. No veteran of the War Between the States ever need buy a ticket to this show, by gorry. Why, she even lets Yankees in, if they be vets."

"Gol," murmured Cotton. "The war was a long time ago. My pa was in it. But he got the measles and almost died. He never did get to fight." Cotton remembered the hours his pa had spent telling him tales of the army.

He was pulled out of his thoughts by Cy yanking on his sleeve.

"Here's Brad, Cotton. Brad, meet my friend, Cotton." His friend? Gol.

Brad was the youngest Bailey brother in the circus. He was twelve, sandy-haired, and played slide trombone. Cy explained that all the boys also doubled as clowns sometimes. And sold tickets. And helped tear down or set up the circus. And fed and groomed some of the animals. Cotton grew tired just thinking of all the work. The circus was evidently not a place for only fun, after all.

The last Bailey that Cotton met caused the flush he so hated to rise from throat to scalp. Her name was Birda, Birda Bailey, and she was the golden-haired girl on Bolivar that first day. She was only nine years old, but she seemed older. Cotton guessed it was from performing before all those people that made her seem so grown-up and sure of herself.

"I'm glad to meet you, Cotton," she said when Cy introduced them and then hustled off, muttering something like "work to do." Cotton hardly noticed him leave.

"Maw told me all about you," Birda added. "Welcome to the Bailey Show. I hope we'll be good friends."

She was tiny and shorter than Cotton, but she held herself straight and tall and moved like she was dancing, even when she wasn't. He wanted to reach out and touch her hair, which was like spun gold and hung halfway to her waist. Her eyes were as blue as the Texas sky, and when she smiled Cotton sort of melted all over.

Birda seemed glad that Cotton had joined the Bailey Show. She smiled and said, "Would you like to see my birds? I'm training them for a new act. We're just about ready."

She led Cotton into the menagerie and crossed to the far side of the tent behind the monkey cages. There, in a big cage, were a dozen or more tiny yellow birds, flittering and chirping. One sat on a little swing and trilled the most beautiful song Cotton had ever heard.

"What kind of birds are these?" he asked, amazed at their vivid yellow color and at the sounds coming from their tiny throats.

"Canaries," Birda said as she made kissing sounds at the birds and spoke to them in a soft voice. "Haven't you ever seen a canary?"

"No'm," answered Cotton, still shy of this pretty creature . . . the one named Birda. "Only birds we had around our place were sparrows and blue jays."

"Well, stand very still and I'll show you something," Birda ordered.

She opened the cage door and put her hand into it. The bird on the swing fluttered down and landed on Birda's finger. Gently she withdrew her hand from the cage.

Instead of flying away as Cotton expected, the little bird performed its tricks, singing when Birda asked it to, hopping on her shoulder and giving her a "kiss." Then Birda brought out another one and the birds played on a miniature teeter-totter and walked tightrope on a bird-sized apparatus.

Cotton could not believe his eyes. Birds were free things, ready to fly away at the first sign of a human getting too near. And here were these little birds obeying Birda's soft-spoken commands.

"I work with all fourteen of them at once in our act," she said, as if reading his mind. "Aren't they wonderful? My pa bought them for me, because I didn't want to work on the high wire or play in the band. I always get lots of applause."

"Cotton! Cotton Bailey! Get yerself over here this minute." It was Cy hollering. Cotton ducked his head at Birda, who was still twittering at her birds, and ran toward Cy's voice.

"Yessir, I'm here, sir."

"It's time to hay up, youngun. Get yerself busy, y'hear? I got no time to be tracking yer down when I needs yer."

His first chore in the circus was haying the bull. He liked knowing the circus lingo — he felt so at home here.

Cotton grabbed a pitchfork and started pitching hay toward Bolivar, who picked it up with his trunk and delivered it to his huge mouth faster than Cotton could get it off the ground. For an hour he worked with the elephant, hauling bucket after bucket of water and pitching more hay.

For his trouble Bolivar rewarded him with a trunkful of water blown skillfully all over Cotton, drenching him. Cotton sputtered, backing away from the elephant's range. He would swear that Bolivar was grinning at him.

"Guess that'll learn ya not to get too close to that old boy, son."

Cotton did not recognize the voice. He wiped the water out of his eyes with his wet sleeve and looked at the voice's owner.

"Hi, I'm Al Bailey, Gus's brother. Makes me uncle to all the Bailey kids. I help train the kinkers and play in the band. Also take tickets and see that we stay Sunday School."

"Sunday School?" Cotton didn't know the circus had any connection to church.

"Yep, that means we run a clean and honest show. No grifters in this show. Aunt Mollie is very strict, you know. Swearin's not allowed. Second offense and you're fired. Drinkin' don't get no second chance. Circus ain't no place for fuzzy heads. Someone could get killed too easy. And if anyone tries to flimflam a spectator . . . ooooeee, they'd better not, all I can say. You never seen Aunt Mollie with her dander up."

Cotton liked Al right away. He must have been about the same age as Aunt Mollie but was easy to talk to. Cotton felt that he had found a new friend.

"Al?" he spoke the man's name with a question in it. He didn't want to seem too forward.

"Yes, son, what you need?" Al's ginger-colored eyes smiled at Cotton even before his mouth did. You can trust someone whose eyes smile, Cotton thought.

"You said you train the kinkers?" At Al's nod he went on. "I was just wondering. Would you train me on the slack wire or trapeze? I'd ever so much like to learn."

Already he could see himself sailing through the air, like the Flying Morenos. His ma and brothers might take notice of him then.

"How old are you, Cotton?"

"Ten, sir."

"You're pretty old to train. We start 'em at six or seven, sometimes even younger. Don't know if it ain't too late for you." Al smiled down at Cotton.

Too old? At ten? All his life everyone had told him he was too young for anything he asked to do. Ma always fussed at him, saying, "You'll get old fast enough, I can tell ya. Don't be wishin' your life away." And now he couldn't do the thing he most wanted in his whole life because he was *too old?*

"Well, son, I can see by the look of ya that your heart's set on bein' a flyer or acrobat. Tell you what. Tomorrow morning around 6:30 come to the ring in the big top and you can watch. I'm trainin' someone now. When you see what hard work it is, you may not want to try. But if you do, we'll give it a whirl." With a nod and a slap on Cotton's back, Al Bailey walked away.

Cotton's heart was pounding. He could try, Al said. Gol, he'd work so hard. He'd show them he wasn't too old.

Then he ran to where Bolivar was chained and started pitching hay as fast as his arms could fly. If he could feed this bull 150 pounds of hay a day and water him besides, he could do anything!

5

The Lessons Begin

Cotton was up before dawn. Aunt Mollie had given him a corner in the bandwagon for his pallet. He liked having this space all to himself. All the Bailey boys crowded into one small living wagon. Other children of the circus lived and traveled with their families. Since Cotton was alone, Aunt Mollie told him he could live in the "special" wagon.

"We bought it right before Gus had to retire," she explained. "It was his pride and joy. Y'see, it looks like a regular wagon, like mine, but the side walls are double and the inside ones can be raised up to reach twenty feet high. When the band sits up there, you can hear them half a county away. 'Course, lots of times Gus cut his lip on his cornet when the wagon lurched on a bump in the road."

"Gol," said Cotton, imagining the red-coated band, their brass horns shining in the sun, sitting high above everyone's heads, playing Mr. Gus's song, "The Old Gray Mare," or Aunt Mollie's favorite, "Dixie."

"We store the band instruments and other equipment in the bandwagon. We can make room for one ten-year-old boy," Aunt Mollie said, her hand resting on Cotton's shoulder.

By now, he was quite at home in his corner of the bandwagon. He stretched to get himself wide awake, then pulled on his clothes. It was very dark inside the wagon, which had only one small window. He slipped out, closing the door quietly so as not to disturb anyone lucky enough to be still asleep in the circle of wagons.

They had not traveled during the night. Al had explained to Cotton: "When we come into a new town where the folks don't know us, we give one show free to everybody. Then we stay over and give another, sellin' tickets, the next day. The first lets folks know what kind of show we run, that it's clean and good for families to see. Most folks have such a good time, they just rush back to buy a ticket the second day."

Cotton thought that was pretty swell, to get to see the circus twice.

He crept through the darkness, past Aunt Mollie's dark wagon and around the menagerie tent. When he got to the big top he heard voices. One of the voices was Al's, friendly and patient. The second voice was a girl's — Birda's?

He walked into the tent, his heart tight in his chest. Was it fear of what he was going to try to do? Or was it the thought of seeing the golden girl again? He didn't know.

"Ah, Cotton! Come on in," called Al. Cotton saw that the girl's voice was not Birda's after all, but belonged to a dark-haired girl, about six inches taller than he. She had the largest, most beautiful eyes he had ever seen. Black, they were, like Aunt Mollie's, but tilted up at the corners a mite. He figured her to be about fifteen, much too old for the likes of him. But gol. . . .

"Cotton, say hello to our next star gymnast, Lotta Moreno. Lotta, this here is Cotton. Cotton Bailey."

The flying trapeze girl!

30

Cotton felt his old demon, the flush, creeping up his neck onto his face and into his hair. He nodded his head, miserable, as the girl Lotta stared at him.

"This towhead is your little brother, Mr. Al?" she asked without acknowledging the introduction.

"Well, no, Maw just named him that when he joined up with the circus. He's wantin' to learn to be an acrobat or aerialist."

Lotta laughed. "A little late, isn't it, to start *now?*"

"Yep, I told him that. But he's a determined young-un, so I told him to come on over this mornin'. We'll show him a few tricks."

Cotton felt like a lump of clay or a fly on the wall, eavesdropping on a conversation that didn't include him. And she called him "towhead." He hated to be called that.

"Well, I'm going up," Lotta said and turned away without ever having spoken directly to Cotton.

He watched as she pulled herself, hand over hand, up the hanging rope, until she reached another rope that ended in a metal ring.

"She's goin' up the web to her position on the rings," Al explained. "Her ma was famous for the one-arm plange, so Lotta is determined to be better at it than her ma was."

"One-armed what?" Cotton asked, his eyes never leaving the tiny figure of Lotta so high above him.

"Plange. Watch her. After she warms up a mite, she'll go into it. She spends hours and hours every day practicing that act. A real determined young lady for only thirteen." Al could not keep the admiration out of his voice.

Only thirteen! That wasn't *too* much older than he was! Gol.

Cotton stood, transfixed, as Lotta went through her paces. She put her hand through the ring and held the rope above it. Then she twisted and turned and threw her body up until she stood on one hand on the ring. She remained in that upside-down position for a few moments. Cotton caught his breath as she dropped back down, looking as though she was going to fall. Instead she swung gracefully back and forth, waving to the "audience."

She is really beautiful, Cotton thought, his heart still pounding from fright. Her olive skin had taken on a glow as she worked, and her dark eyes shone with lights that flashed like little diamonds. The blue satin bloomers, tights, and shirtwaist she wore made her look like a bluebird, high in the sky, Cotton thought. As he watched, Lotta moved to another rope, this one with a velvet loop at the end, instead of a metal ring.

"See, Cotton," Al was saying. "She is about to start the plange. She will slip her right wrist through the loop which is attached to a swivel. D'ya see?"

Cotton could only nod as Lotta started throwing her body back and forth, getting up speed. It was the same thing Cotton did on the swing in the backyard — except that she was many feet above the ground, hanging by one wrist.

He knew she was getting ready for the one-armed whatever. He held his breath.

She hurled her body into a full circle over itself, over and over again, her arm acting as the swivel. Cotton had never seen anything like it. The girl's body swung through the air, swooping as gracefully as a swallow, her long, loose hair a dark cloud following her through each arc. In the silent tent he could hear her laugh as joyously as a child on a backyard swing.

At that moment, Cotton lost his heart to her.

The spirals slowed, Lotta caught the web with her foot and gracefully glided down the rope to the floor. She raised her long hair from her neck, and Cotton could see the beads of perspiration on her throat and face. He rushed toward her, to tell her how wonderful she was, but he didn't get the chance.

Without a glance his way, she slipped into her shoes and robe and left the tent.

"Gol . . ." Cotton whispered to himself.

"She's somethin' pretty special, ain't she?" Al said with a grin.

"Gol . . ." was all Cotton could get out.

"Well, boy, let's see what you can do now." Al was all business.

Would he have to climb the "web"? Or swing on the trapeze that lazily dangled high overhead? Cotton felt a tremor of fear sweep through him.

"Ah, there you are, Al." It was Aunt Mollie's voice and she followed it into the tent . . . "top," that is, Cotton reminded himself. He was a little ashamed of how relieved he was to have his "lesson" interrupted.

"Oh, good mornin', Cotton. I wondered where you had got to so early," Aunt Mollie said with a smile.

"Yes'm, I asked Mr. Al if I could learn to be an acrobat or something. I'll just go along and feed Bolivar now."

Al laughed. "He just watched Lotta go through her paces. Scared him a mite, I reckon."

"Don't be afraid, Cotton. Al won't ask you to do anything you're not ready for. Show him what you want him to practice on, Al, then come with me. I want to talk to you about those loafers we saw hangin' around the top yesterday. I don't want a clem to start and ruin the show."

With a look at Cotton, who was thoroughly confused, she explained. "A 'clem,' Cotton, is a fight. Sometimes tough fellows think they can break up the circus and start bullyin' and pushin' their way in without payin'. If you ever hear someone yell, 'Hey, Rube,' that's the circus call that there's a clem startin'. Everybody joins in and cleans the bullies out. If you hear 'Hey, Rube,' grab a stick and come runnin', y'hear?" She reached into the depths of the large black bag she always carried. "Here's a white kerchief to put around your neck, so's everyone on our side will know you're circus folk and not one of the ruffians."

Cotton felt his chest swell with pride. Aunt Mollie

treated him as if he was a man, instead of a little old ten-year-old.

"Yes'm, Aunt Mollie," he said, his eyes shining. "I'll fight those bullies, yes'm, I will."

"Good," Aunt Mollie said as she left the tent. "Al, give this boy a ten-minute lesson, then come to my wagon."

"Right, Mollie," Al said. "C'mon, Cotton, let's get to work."

Cotton's mind was still on the clem and how he would finish off those bullies. He forgot to be afraid of what Al was going to expect of him. He stepped over the dirt ring and walked to the center.

"Whoa, Cotton, back out of there," Al hollered. "You came into the ring wrong foot first. You have to enter the ring right foot forward. Left foot, like you did, is bad luck for the circus. You don't want to bring us bad luck, do ya?"

Horrified that he might be the deliverer of bad luck to the circus and Aunt Mollie, Cotton backed up so fast he almost fell down. Carefully, he placed his right foot over the ring. He glanced up at Al, who was grinning at him.

"Good boy. You'll find out we circus folk have lots of funny ways. Peacocks or their feathers are bad luck. And, if you put on your underwear wrong side out, don't change it before bedtime. You tempt fate if you do. Now, if you should see three white horses and *no* red-haired woman, that's mighty good luck. Y'see?"

"Yessir," Cotton said, trying to memorize which brought good luck and which brought bad.

"All right, we're ready to start your first lesson," Al said with a get-down-to-business tone in his voice.

"First, I want you to watch me and then see if you can do what I do."

Cotton, his nerves taut, got ready to climb the web.

Instead, Al was doing a series of bending exercises.

Gol, was that all? That was baby stuff. He followed Al's lead and waited for the next step.

"Do those every day, and when you're ready we'll go on," Al said as he walked off to meet Aunt Mollie.

Cotton had never felt so let down. He had had visions, a little fearfully perhaps, of swinging on the trapeze or from the rings, of showing the elegant Lotta that he could do something too.

Gol, she'd laugh if she saw him doing these baby exercises.

"Oh, Cotton, how lovely. You're going to be an acrobat?" The voice was Birda's. She skipped up to where Cotton, red-faced, was in the middle of a deep knee bend.

Compared to Lotta, Birda suddenly looked very young and awkward, like a child. Cotton decided that she would make a very nice younger sister. The butterflies that had churned his stomach when he met her were all gone.

"Yep, Birda," he said with an ease that surprised him. She was just a little nine-year-old girl, after all. "Al's going to teach me some routines. He didn't have time today, so he had me doing these easy bends."

"Oh, Cotton, they're not just 'easy bends.' They're a very important part of training to be an acrobat," Birda explained. "You have to learn timing and total coordination. It will be months before you're ready for the trapeze. Next you'll do handstands or roll-overs and flip-flops. Then Al will advance you to somersaults."

"Gol, I been doing somersaults since I was five years old!" Cotton couldn't hold back his disappointment that so much time should be wasted, when he wanted to get up there, high under the top, and show Lotta what he could do.

"This is different. You'll see. I watched my brother Allie train to go on the slack wire. I was very small then, but I decided I didn't want any part of it. That's why I work with Bolivar and train my canaries." Birda smiled at Cotton and waved her hand as she left him alone in the big top.

Dejected, he did several more bends and then started

for the menagerie tent to feed Bolivar. At least that was man's work, not this baby stuff.

He finished his chores, went to the mess tent for breakfast, and watched the band practice for the afternoon performance. His job would be to stand at the entrance of the big top with Aunt Mollie and greet folks as they came in. "Howdy, folks, nice to see you," Aunt Mollie would say to each one. She would be dressed in her heavy, dark silk gown and wear her hair piled high on her head. At her throat she would wear a jeweled pin, a "garnet," she called it. Mr. Gus had given it to her when they had started their own circus, she said, after so many years of doing other things. She had always dreamed of the circus.

"We were the Bailey Family Troupe, at first. Just Gus and Al and my sister Fanny and me. Fanny is no longer with us, but I don't know how I'd manage without Al. He reminds me some of my Gus, but younger and not as red-headed. Gus is ten years older than I am. And such a sweetheart. You'd like him, my Gus."

When Aunt Mollie started talking about the "old days" and "my Gus," her eyes got a faraway look. Cotton knew that she wasn't talking to him, but to herself. It just helped to have him there, he thought. He liked hearing about the early days of the Bailey family.

"Then, of course, the War Between the States happened, and we took Fanny and our baby Dixie to a friend's home in Richmond. Then Gus, Al, and I joined Hood's Texas Brigade."

Cotton looked at Aunt Mollie with questions in his eyes.

"Well, of course, I didn't join. I became a nurse and also helped the men in the Hood's minstrels and did some entertainin'. Those boys in gray sure did love it when I played my lap organ and sang for them.

"Someday I'll tell you about how I became a Confederate spy, Cotton. But now it's time to greet the folks."

Cotton's eyes grew wide at the thought of Aunt Mollie as a *spy*.

"Howdy, glad to see you back again today, ma'am." Aunt Mollie was all smiles and shook each and every one's hand.

Nearly all the ticket holders had filed into the big top when Cotton heard a ruckus at the ticket booth. A burly fellow with a booming voice was yelling at Al, who was taking tickets.

"You circus trash is all alike! Out to rob us, take our money, and then sneak away in the middle of the night." He shook his fist at Al. "Wall, yez ain't gittin' away with it this time. We're goin' in, and we're not payin', see? Whatcherz goin' to do about it, eh?"

He swaggered away from the booth, and Al leaped over the half-door of the ticket wagon, after him.

Before Cotton could have counted three, if he had thought to count, fists were flying . . . not only Al's and the burly stranger's, but also those of a half-dozen others who had joined him.

"Hey, Rube!" Al yelled at the top of his voice.

That was the signal!

From all over the circus, Cotton heard the cry, picked up and echoed.

"Hey, Rube!"

He pulled his white kerchief out of his pocket, and with shaking fingers tied it around his neck. Out of the corner of his eye he could see the circus people running toward the trouble spot.

"Hey, Rube!"

Gol, he was going to get to do something grown-up after all. He was going to be part of his first "clem"!

6

Indians Coming!

"I should never have encouraged him. He just yearns so to be grown-up. I never dreamed we'd really have a clem today!"

It was Aunt Mollie's voice, coming from a long way off.

"Don't fret yourself, Mollie. He'll be right as rain real soon. He's a plucky little fella."

That sounded like Al.

"Maw, I do wish he'd open his eyes and say something to us. I'm so worried about him."

Birda.

Why were they all talking about him again, as though he wasn't there? Just like Lotta did. Lotta. Where was she? He didn't hear her voice. Maybe if he opened his eyes. . . .

"Oh, there you are, Cotton," Aunt Mollie spoke in the cheery, loud voice people used on sick folks. "How's your head feelin'?"

His head. Somewhere up there he had a head, he knew it. But for now he didn't even want to think about it. If he did, the pain would start again. And it was the pain that made everything go black.

"The clem?" he asked in what sounded to him like a very small child's voice.

"Over and done with," came Al's hearty reply. "We trounced those ruffians good. Too bad you got a lick the first go, Cotton. You didn't get a chance to get in the fight."

Over with. The fight was over with. And he did nothing but get a board bounced off his head! He couldn't seem to do anything right.

"That's all right, Cotton," Birda's soft voice had a soothing effect on him. "We're all proud of you. You acted very bravely, didn't he, Maw?"

"Yes, indeed he did. Now, we're goin' to get out of here and let you rest, Cotton. Soon's you know it, you'll be good as new."

With that, they all left him alone with his thoughts. Lotta had not been there to see how he was. He couldn't swing on the trapeze. He couldn't even fight in his first clem. He was a failure. Lotta was prob'ly laughing at him right now.

Days passed swiftly in the circus. There was never enough time to do everything in one day. On performance days Cotton helped unpack the gear from the wagons and place the poles around the lot in the proper positions for the tent. He helped lug the canvas out and unroll it, then lash it to bale rings at the center pole which lay on the ground. Cy and the other roughnecks drove stakes into the ground with sixteen-pound sledge hammers. At Cy's signal, men and horses heaved and pulled and, as if by magic, the center pole was lifted upright and the canvas with it. In a matter of minutes the huge tent was in place, tied to the stakes, and the roughnecks were hauling in the blues and setting them up around the big top.

After the day's show, it had to be done all over again,

only in the opposite direction. Everything had to be knocked down, packed, and hauled to the next show town.

Then there was school. Cotton felt keen disappointment when he learned that he hadn't escaped going to school by joining the circus. Every morning Aunt Mollie gave lessons to all the circus younguns. She was a strict schoolmarm and expected her students to have their work done, no matter what!

Somehow Cotton found time to do his exercises every day. He was up to somersaults now. Sometimes he caught sight of Lotta, practicing on the rings. She barely acknowledged his presence. At performances he always watched her and her family, the Flying Morenos, with awe and envy. Someday he'd show her — and his ma — what he could do.

One morning, when the circus was in West Texas, Aunt Mollie sent for Cotton to come to her living wagon. He hurried from the menagerie tent to the red wagon that was full of memories for him.

"Yes'm, Aunt Mollie?"

"Cotton, dear, I want you to paper the next town for me."

"Pardon?"

"Oh, I'm sorry. I forget there are things you still haven't learned about the circus." Aunt Mollie brushed Cotton's light hair out of his eyes. "You're to take the circus posters on to Sterling City and tack 'em up. You'll ride horseback and leave now, so the folks will be ready for us when we get there day after tomorrow. You can easily get to Sterling City and back by nightfall, if you hurry."

Cotton's chest swelled. At last. Something he could do to prove he was a man, not just a little kid.

"Here's the packet of posters, Cotton," Aunt Mollie said, "and tacks, a hammer, and this package of leather pieces. Be sure to put a little piece of leather between paper and tack. Keeps the paper from tearin' and fallin' off before folks can read it. Wind's pretty strong out here. Remember now, y'hear?"

"Yes'm, I will, I promise."

"Good. Well, get along with you so's you can get back before dark. Oh, yes, stop at any ranches near town that have big barns and tell the ranchers they get free lifetime passes if we can paint a billboard on the side of their barns."

"Yes'm. Well, 'bye," Cotton said, anxious to get on his way.

"Oh, and Cotton," Aunt Mollie added, "be sure to paper the livery stable. That's one place the ruffians don't dare tear down our posters. Blacksmith doesn't allow rough carryin's on around his place."

"Yes'm." Cotton hesitated, waiting for further last-minute instructions from Aunt Mollie.

"Well, what are you waitin' for? Get goin', y'hear?"

Grinning, Cotton ran to where the horses were tied behind the menagerie tent. He picked his favorite, a gray mare named Gretel, saddled her, and jumped on her back, clutching his parcel of posters.

He hoped that Lotta caught sight of him, riding out of camp on an important mission for Aunt Mollie.

" 'Bye, Cotton," a girl's voice rang out. He twisted in the saddle to see.

Oh. It was just Birda.

" 'Bye," he answered without too much enthusiasm.

The folks in Sterling City were most friendly. Aunt Mollie had been showing there for years, and all she had to do was write the date for the next performance on last year's poster, or even send a plain sheet with "Aunt Mollie's comin'!" on it and the date below. Everyone would show up to meet the first of the wagons before daybreak, turn out for the parade, and then line up early for the afternoon show. He put up all his "paper" and turned back the way he had come.

It was nearly sundown, that violet time of day when everything in West Texas takes on a soft rosy glow. Cotton was daydreaming in the saddle, moseying along at Gretel's own pace. Only a half-mile more to go.

Something moving caught his eye in the far corner of his vision.

Indians!

A single file of them, on horseback, slowly descending a hill not too far from where Cotton reckoned the circus would be camped. He'd better hurry and beat them there. No telling if they were friendly Indians or not. He dug his heels into Gretel's side. She began to trot. At his insistence she was soon galloping at full speed, Cotton hanging on with both hands, letting her have her head. He knew she would find the quickest path home. It was dinner time.

He kept an eye on the Indians, hoping they were not doing the same with him. They kept a steady pace, slow and easy, down the far side of the hill. If he could just gain camp before they rounded the curve at the base of the hill, they might not spot him.

He and Gretel reached the circle of wagons and raced, full-speed, into the center of them. Dogs and children scattered, and one or two women screeched in fright.

"Where's Aunt Mollie?" he demanded.

"In her wagon doing her books," the first woman answered without taking time to fuss at him for scaring them.

Cotton jumped down off Gretel and ran around the circle until he spotted Aunt Mollie's red wagon. Without knocking, he burst through the door. Aunt Mollie looked up from her little desk in the corner and laughed.

"Well, Cotton, you look like I felt when I was riding away from Yankee camp and just knew those bluecoats were after me! What's the trouble?"

"Indians . . . Indians!" was all Cotton could get out. He gasped for breath. "They're coming down the far side of the hill out there. I saw 'em and raced home to beat 'em. Do you think they're going to attack us, Aunt Mollie?"

"Well, Cotton, I guess we'll just have to wait and see about that. Meantime, I have a little friend here that may scare them off." She dug in her trunk and pulled out an old pistol, the kind used in the war. "It was Gus's," she explained as she expertly loaded the gun. "Now, come on. Let's see about these Indians."

They left the wagon and Cotton led Aunt Mollie to where she could see the first of the Indians coming around the bend.

"Don't recognize the tribe," she said. "Guess we better not take chances. Cotton, you go and warn everyone. They need to blow out all the lights. Have Cy douse the torches. Tell the women and children to hide in the wagons and the men to stand by. I don't allow my people to carry guns, so I reckon it's up to me to scare these Indians off. Go on now."

Cotton ran through the campsite, telling everyone in a quiet, firm voice to hide and stay still. Within seconds the place was deserted, the circus people disappearing as though by magic. Cotton ran back to Aunt Mollie.

She was sitting on an overturned half-barrel, her gun propped on a wagon wheel. She didn't speak to Cotton, only nodded to let him know he had done well.

"They're starting to circle the camp," she whispered after a few silent moments. "Doesn't look good."

The sky was nearly dark now, just a last tint of royal blue along the horizon. The last of the sunset's colors had disappeared below the earth's edge.

Cotton shivered. Indians liked to attack after dark. He closed his eyes, then jumped like a rabbit when he heard the gunshot right next to him.

It was Aunt Mollie's pistol. She had shot three or four times into the air.

"That ought to scare 'em off," she said. "Cotton, crawl under the wagon here and see if you can spot 'em. Are they runnin' away?"

"No'm, Aunt Mollie, they're still closing up the circle around us."

Cotton could not remember ever being so frightened. He didn't want to die. He'd never see Ma or Annie again. He hadn't even gotten up on the trapeze yet. He hadn't proven to himself — or to Lotta — that he could do it.

"Do you s'pose they're planning to scalp us?"

"Not if Mollie Bailey can help it," she declared. "Come on, Cotton, I have another idea."

Cotton hoped it was something they could do in a hurry, because the Indians were getting closer and closer. For a long moment he closed his eyes, but he knew that wouldn't make the savages go away. He opened them again. Aunt Mollie was halfway across the open area, hurrying toward his wagon. What could she be doing? He ran after her.

"Hurry up, Cotton," she said as he caught up with her. "I'm goin' to need your help with this."

With what? Cotton wondered, mystified.

Aunt Mollie lifted up her skirts and seemed to fly up the steps to the bandwagon where Cotton slept. She pushed open the door and motioned Cotton to follow.

"Here," she said, "help me with this. We'll take it outside. Quickly now."

She pushed band instrument cases out of the way and reached to the back wall of the wagon.

The big bass drum! What did she want with that?

Cotton hurried to give her a hand, wondering if Aunt Mollie's mind was playing tricks on her, what with Indians about to attack and all.

They heaved and hauled the big drum out to the open field surrounded by the little circle of wagons. The men, outside again, milled around, brandishing their "Hey Rube" clubs and sticks in defiance of the advancing Indians. Cotton thought that they prob'ly wished for a few rifles right about now.

When the drum was set up, Aunt Mollie said to Cotton, "Well, boy, let's see how the Indians like this!"

44

With a flourish she took the big drum stick and began to beat on the drum, as hard as she could.

Boom! Boom! Boom!

The sound bounced off the wagons and on into the hills.

Boom! Boom! Boom!

"Hurry, Cotton," Aunt Mollie whispered, as though the Indians might hear her, "crawl beneath the wagon there and see what the Indians are doin'."

Cotton lay on his stomach and scooted underneath the wagon. He peeked out into the darkness.

The Indians were leaving! Riding at a gallop back toward the hill!

"They're going, they're going, Aunt Mollie! You did it. You scared the Indians away!" Cotton jumped up from the ground and hugged Aunt Mollie.

"I figured they'd be a mite scared of a "cannon" like they have at the fort. They know what damage one of those big boys can do. Call 'em 'thunder wagons.' I just had to hope they'd be fooled by my drummin'!" Aunt Mollie hugged Cotton back, and then brushed her skirts and smoothed her hair into place.

"It's all right, everyone. You can come out now. The Indians are gone, scared by our old circus drum!"

7

The Confederate Spy

As a reward for Cotton's part in the Indian rout, Aunt Mollie invited him to accompany her into town to buy supplies and hand out small pamphlets about the circus. They would also give free tickets to the mayor and officials of Sterling City, as well as to the sheriff and his deputies.

"It helps to keep the big boys happy. Sometimes the fee for showin' in their town gets cut down a mite. Never hurts to have friends in high places."

Cotton wore his best clothes to town, painfully squeezing into the Sunday shoes he had not worn since joining the circus. Gol, he had grown!

Cy hitched Aunt Mollie's favorite black horse, Mariah, to her jaunty little black cart. Its two giant wheels and side-lanterns made it the spiffiest carriage Sterling City had ever seen, Cotton reckoned. He sat tall and straight, proud of the cart and proud of Aunt Mollie. She was dressed in a black dress, made of some shiny stuff that swished as she walked, and a black bonnet tied under her chin. As always, she wore her garnet pin at her throat. Cotton didn't know about such things, but he thought Aunt Mollie was the most elegant lady he had ever seen.

"C'mon, Cotton, we've some shopping to do first." Aunt Mollie was all business. She took out her list and entered the general store.

"Mornin', sir," she said with that warm smile of hers. "I'm Mollie Bailey, with the circus outside of town. You're new here, I believe?"

"Yes, ma'am, I am. Bought out Joe Murray last winter. I'm Ralph Eberhart. Folks just call me Eb."

"And folks just call me Aunt Mollie, Eb. Pleased to make your acquaintance. This is my boy, Cotton."

Cotton ducked his head, feeling the red rising of his flush. Aunt Mollie had called him her "boy." Gol.

Aunt Mollie started on her shopping list, naming one thing at a time.

"Two barrels of flour, please, Eb," she said.

"Yes'm. What else can I get you?"

"Give me the cost of the flour, Eb. I'll pay for that first. Then we'll get on with the list. I pay as I go."

Cotton watched as Aunt Mollie bought supplies for the circus, paying for each one as Eb plunked it on the counter. She reached into her old black bag time after time and patiently waited for change.

"Here, Cotton, while I'm doin' this shoppin' you can pass these pamphlets out. Go down Main Street and give 'em to everyone you see. Then come back here, and we'll fit you up with some shoes that won't pinch your toes off."

She handed Cotton a stack of cards printed on both sides.

As he walked down the street, handing the cards to everyone he met, he began to read one. On the front of the card was a picture of Aunt Mollie's strong face with the slightest of smiles. Under the picture was printed:

Just a few lines to say that I will be back among my old friends once again and I hope to see all the familiar faces of last year, and to make new friends. They may be assured of a hearty welcome. My company this year is excellent.

Yours lovingly,
Mollie A. Bailey
WHY NOT SPREAD THE NEWS?

On the opposite side, Cotton read with growing amazement:

A Confederate Spy

Prominent among those noble women who buckled on the armor and belted the sword was one who rode with the brave Texans, who did scout duty and still more perilous work as a spy in the enemy's camp. A true heroine, she smuggled packets of quinine, hidden in her hair, through enemy lines, to our boys in the Third Arkansas, Hood's Texas Brigade. Posing as an old lady selling cookies, she boldly entered the enemy's camp, gleaning military information from the Yankee soldiers' loose talk.

Cotton hunched up his trousers and brushed his hair out of his eyes. He read on:

Young, beautiful and tender, she was as brave and as loyal to her country as the truest boy in jacket of gray that ever fought with Lee and Jackson, marched with Jeb Stuart, or rode with Morgan's raiders, and her service was as valuable as it was valiant.

This noble and remarkable woman — this Confederate spy — this Southland heroine — is none other than Mollie Bailey. . . .

This tribute is but poor praise of her peerless worth, but is a freewill offering from one who holds in sacred respect the story of the Southland's Lost Cause.

There was more, but Cotton could only see the picture of Aunt Mollie, a young lady from a fine Alabama plantation who had risked her life for her country. She *was* a true heroine.

All the way home Cotton was quiet, deep in thought, wondering if he could ever accomplish half as much for the good of others as Aunt Mollie had already done. Gol, she was somethin' special.

He helped her unload the cart and started toward his wagon, clutching his new shoes, to change his clothes. He saw Al coming toward him.

"Hi, Mr. Al," he called.

"Howdy, Cotton. Just wanted you to know that startin' tomorra you'll be practicin' on the trap."

Remembering that "trap" was circus talk for trapeze, Cotton gulped. Was he ready? Would he have the courage to climb to the highest point in the top? Or the ability to learn timing and the dozen other things Al said he needed before he could fly?

All he could do was stammer, "Gol, thanks, Mr. Al."

Tomorrow . . . it would be his test. He closed his eyes. Nope, he was still afraid, might as well admit it.

Well, he knew one thing for sure. He wouldn't let Lotta see him afraid. No, sir. Not him. He'd be as brave as Aunt Mollie was when she rode into the enemy camp, spying on the Yankees.

8

Up, Up in the Air
— Almost

Cotton put on the practice costume Al had given him. It was a soft shirt with full sleeves and belt at the waist. He pulled on silk tights and slippers.

"Gol, I feel like a girl wearing stockings," he complained, embarrassed. He thought how his brothers Joe and Will would taunt him if they could see him dressed like this.

"Everyone feels like that at first," Al said. "You have a French fellow named Jules Leotard to blame for the tights. He developed them for kinkers after he changed the trapeze from stationary to one, like ours, that swings. That was back in '59, Cotton, so there's been lots of fellas since then that have felt like you do.

"Here, put this on and fasten it so's it won't come off. It could save your life."

Al handed Cotton a wide leather beltlike contraption with ropes attached to rings on each side. Cotton fastened it around his waist and then looked at Al.

"What is it? What're the ropes for?"

"It's called a 'mechanic' and all kinkers wear it while

trainin'. The ropes run through pulleys high up under the top ceiling and back down to me. If you should fall from the trap, the mechanic will keep you aloft, swingin' like a puppet on a string until I let you down."

Cotton had turned pale at Al's mention of falling.

"Don't worry none, boy. I won't let you hit the tanbark. Now, let's get up there and see how you do."

Al showed Cotton how to shinny up the web, hand-over-hand like he used to climb the willow tree out back at home. Lotta's brother, Leo, stood on the small platform, waiting to help Cotton onto the trapeze.

Leo was slight of build but had the broadest shoulders and neck Cotton had ever seen. Must be from all that swinging on the trap, Cotton thought, and catching hold of his papa's hands in midair.

Leo's smile was encouraging, although he did not speak. It was up to Al, as Cotton's "patter" or coach, to tell Cotton what to do.

"Cotton," Al spoke in a normal tone even though Cotton was high above him, "stand straight on the platform, facing the other trap. Good. Now Leo will unhook your trap from the rigging and you take the two ropes in your hands with the flybar directly in front of you.

"When you feel 'right,' step out onto the bar and lower yourself to a sitting position. Timing is everything here. Your instincts will tell when to go and when to stay."

Leo unfastened the trap and handed the ropes to Cotton, whose mouth was as dry as his name. His heart was beating so hard, he knew Al could hear it down there on the ground.

How he wished he were on that safe, old ground right now.

When he put his left foot onto the bar, it jerked away from him. He pulled his foot back and nearly lost his balance. If only the little platform were bigger, he wished.

"Leo, show Cotton how to get on the trap, will you?" Al called.

"Right, Al," Leo said, as he took the ropes back.

Cotton grasped the platform's pole for dear life. How he wished he could slide down it, and never, never get himself up here again. For a moment he closed his eyes.

"Watch Leo," Al said to Cotton. "See how he raises his body a little bit and just sort of slides onto the flybar, lettin' his hands come down the ropes to a comfortable position. Now let Cotton try again, Leo."

He knew he had to do it. Whatever had made him think he wanted to do this?

Oh no, he thought. Lotta had come in and she was glancing up to see who was on the rigging. He'd die if he disgraced himself now.

Without another thought he lifted his weight from the platform and slid his hands down the ropes till his bottom touched the bar. He had done it!

Leo let go of the trapeze, and Cotton was carried out over the net and up and back and up and back.

He had done it! He was on the trapeze, swinging just like the Flying Morenos. Gol, it felt the same as his swing at home, only higher. Nothing to it.

He looked down in triumph. He wanted to see Al's face and, more, he wanted to see what Lotta thought about his being up here, just like one of them.

Al was grinning and shaking his two hands together in congratulations. Lotta had wandered away and was talking to her father. She hadn't even stayed to watch him, his very first time out on the swing.

"That's great, Cotton," Al called, pride in his voice. "Now, every day you'll get up there and swing for a couple of hours. Try to get a feel of the timing of the back and forth strokes of the trap. It will be the most important thing you'll learn as an aerialist."

So this was all he would be allowed to do. For how long? Another two months? Disappointment rushed over him. He had expected to get a flying lesson tomorrow. He'd never get to perform and show Lotta how good he was.

With Al coaching him, he pulled himself up to a

standing position, then carefully turned on the bar to face Leo. On the next backswing Leo caught the ropes and brought Cotton up to the platform. He put his other hand out and caught Cotton's arm, pulling him off the trapeze and onto the platform again.

"Nice work, boy," Leo said. Then, with the effortless grace Cotton so admired, he jumped off the platform, did a somersault in midair, and landed on his back on the net, bouncing high into the air and coming down on his feet. He finally grabbed the edge of the net and did a roll-off to the ground.

"Er . . . thanks," Cotton said, too late.

How awkward he felt as he timidly let himself down the web, sliding and stopping with jerks and starts.

"Well, Cotton, how did it feel up there?"

It was Aunt Mollie and Birda was with her, standing a little apart, smiling shyly at him.

"It was pretty swell, Aunt Mollie. I liked it," he said, forgetting all about his moments of fear.

"You were wonderful, Cotton," Birda said. "You'll make a fine flyer one day."

"Thanks," Cotton said, his eyes turning toward where Lotta still stood with her father, Leo, Sr. She did not look his way.

Disappointed, he ran to the dressing tent behind the big top and changed into his everyday clothes.

His first day as an aerialist was over.

53

9

A Flyer At Last

It was Saturday, pay day. Aunt Mollie paid the workmen on Wednesdays and the kinkers on Saturdays. Cotton was proud to be included with the performers.

Each week he took three of the four dollars he earned and sent it to his ma, with a note about his life in the circus. He hoped it helped her make ends meet; he never heard a word from her.

The dollar he kept was his own and he used it, sometimes wisely, sometimes foolishly, however his fancy decided.

He loved to be able to saunter up to the candy butcher and pay for cotton candy or to the lemonade booth and order a pink lemonade from old Elroy, who'd been traveling with Aunt Mollie for years.

"Yer likes that lemonade, don't yerz?" Elroy, toothless, would gum.

"Yep," answered Cotton, his mouth full of the sweet/tart taste.

"Did I ever tell yer how pink lemonade came about?" Elroy didn't wait for Cotton's shake of the head. "Was back in '57, I thinks. A fella name of Pete Conklin did it, accidental like.

"He had an old covered wagon and two old mules and he bought himself some tartaric acid, sugar, and one lemon. He always carried this lemon with him and let 'er float on top so's ever'body would get the idee that the lemonade were made with it, yer see. That old lemon was good for many a show, floatin' on top.

"Well, one day it were extra hot, and the folks be extra thirsty. Pete ran out of lemonade. Seems the animals were extra thirsty too, 'cause the circus had plumb run out of water. The thirsty folks wuz hollerin' for their lemonade. Pete ran into the nearest tent, lookin' for water, and there, by gorry, were a big pot of water just a sittin' there. He grabbed it up and threw his lemonade together, floated his lemon on top, and was back in business.

"Don'cher know, when he poured out the first glass, it were *pink!* Pete couldn't figger what had happened to it, but bein' the businessman that he were, he just yelled out, 'Pink lemonade! Get yer pink lemonade here!' Sold out in nothin' flat, he did. Folks seemed to like it Pete's way."

Cotton laughed and sipped his drink.

"How did it get pink, Elroy?"

"Funny thing, boy. Pete asked the kinkers in that tent why the water had been pink. Seems that the bareback rider had washed her red tights and rinsed 'em in that pot. The pink had bled out of them tights!"

"Oh, yuk!" Cotton looked at his lemonade, as pink as you please. He poured it out on the ground.

"Oh, no trouble nowadays, son. We just put a little red color in. Here, let me give you another glass. On the house."

"No thanks, Elroy. I've had enough for now," Cotton said, heading for the menagerie to hay the bull.

Autumn had flown by, and now winter would soon

catch up with them. The circus was on its last round of South Texas. By December it would arrive in Houston, new winter quarters, and stay there. The wagons would be stored in a vacant lot near the house Aunt Mollie had bought. There they would be repaired and repainted, all slicked up for the spring season. Mr. Gus was already living in the new house, the warmer climate being better for his health.

Most of the circus people would leave and go to their permanent homes for the winter, returning in time to start out on the road in April.

Cotton was unsure what his future would be with the Mollie Bailey Show. He did so want to remain with Aunt Mollie and all the circus people. But she had told Ma she'd keep him until they got back to Huntsville. Would he have to go home, back to a dull, unhappy life? Or did Aunt Mollie plan to keep him with her?

One day as he headed for the big top to practice his trap swings, his spirits sagged. He supposed Aunt Mollie would send him home. Gol. And he prob'ly wouldn't even get a chance to perform in the circus, before he got sent away!

He had done so well too. Al had let him do some simple tricks, and he had found that the months of training had been worth it. He was ready for whatever Al would throw at him.

Now when he climbed the web, he did it gracefully. He knew to stand on the platform and wave one arm to the audience, a big smile on his face. After his practice sessions, he was able to leap down into the net, land on his back, bounce to his feet, and make a quick descent to the ground.

He was a flyer.

Aunt Mollie had made him a costume of flashing white with silver spangles. The top fit snugly to his body and the tights were spangled to match. He had never worn it. It waited in the costume tent for the day Al would say he was ready to perform before people in the big top.

How he yearned for that day.

Leo was his catcher, the one who dangled his head down from the second trapeze, called the catchbar. His job was to catch Cotton in his flight from the flybar into midair.

Cotton stood on the platform and wiped his sweaty palms with the resin bag. He looked at Al for the signal to start. Al nodded.

Leo said, in his patient voice, "Now, Cotton, it's time for your layout."

He had just learned the trick and was still a bit nervous about it. But the months of practice had given him self-confidence.

Leo's brother Nino had taken his place on the platform to hand Cotton the flybar and to assist him on his return.

Cotton held tight to the flybar, waiting for Leo's signal.

"Go!" called Leo.

Cotton leaped forward and pumped his body upward and back, gaining momentum. He raised his legs horizontally in front of himself to the "pike" position, pointing his toes.

Leo called, "Break!"

Cotton, feeling like an eagle, so sure of himself, flung his legs upward and released the bar. He soared into a backward somersault.

Leo swung forward to meet him, his arms outstretched. Cotton felt the reassuring, solid grip of Leo's hands around his wrists.

"You did it!" Leo's voice had a ring of pride in it.

Together they swung for a moment. Then Leo released his hold and Cotton flew across and grabbed the flybar.

He landed on the platform, Nino steadying him. With a flourish, Cotton bowed low to the "crowd."

Al applauded and yelled, "Bravo, Cotton!"

He was back down on the ground, drying himself off, when Al said, "I think you're ready, Cotton. How about doin' that trick for our last show of the season, before we break for winter quarters?"

Cotton's heart soared as high as the little platform so far above him. He was ready! Now he could prove to Ma that he was a man. And show Lotta that he could fly with the best of them. Maybe someday he'd be the star performer, with his face on posters, and folks would come from miles around just to see him — Cotton Bailey. Then maybe Lotta would come to him and ask to be his partner, and they could do all the difficult tricks plus a few of their own.

Cotton's daydream was cut short.

"Cotton, you were wonderful up there. You're so brave!" It was Birda, her golden hair tied with a blue bow that matched the blue of her eyes. Cotton had to admit, she looked mighty pretty.

Birda gazed at him in admiration. He felt himself growing taller and bigger. It was a nice feeling.

Then Lotta stood beside him, her beauty enough to make him catch his breath.

"So you've learned to fly, Cotton," she said, with a small smile.

Gol, she knew his name, after all! Never had she spoken it, till now.

"Al says you're going to perform with us for the last show. I think that's very nice."

As he ducked his head in confusion, he caught a glimpse of Birda, walking away. He looked at Lotta. Why did her few, casual words mean more to him than everyone else's compliments? He felt himself blushing, but for once he didn't care. Lotta had told him she liked him, hadn't she?

He could fly right off the ground, he thought, without a flybar, without a trap. Lotta had spoken to him, had encouraged him.

Life was the best it could ever be, he thought later, as he stripped off his practice outfit and climbed back into his work clothes. For the first time, he regarded the tights with respect and love. They were part of his new life, his life as a flyer.

Surely now, now that he could fly, Aunt Mollie would want him to stay.

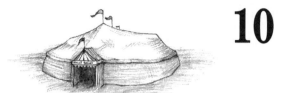

10

Cotton's Big Day

For four days rain had dampened spirits and lowered ticket sales for the Mollie Bailey Show. It had become a contest between Mother Nature and Cy and his roughnecks. The worse the weather, the harder and better they worked — to set up camp, to locate the big top where the wind was least apt to surprise it with a blowdown, to herd the animals into shelter before they panicked at lightning and thunder.

Cotton admired the roustabout crew's dedication more each bad day that passed.

Just getting to the next town had become a challenge. Slogging along in ankle-deep mud, the horses tired sooner than in dry weather. When a wagon got stuck in the mud, or worse, turned over, the patient crew labored for hours with the overworked horses to get the wagon safely back on course. Sometimes Bolivar had to be brought up to use his great strength. When that happened, everyone piled out of their wagons, rain or no rain, to watch the big bull work.

Before the last kinker had joined the crowd cheering

him on, Bolivar would have hauled the wagon up from the ditch full of mud or pulled the overturned wagon upright once again. Cheers for Bolivar! The circus people, drenched but laughing and singing, would return to their wagons and set out again on their way.

On one such morning, before the dawn that no one could see through the angry clouds, Cotton had been routed out of bed by the cry, "Halt the train! Wagon down!"

Sleepily, he peeked out of his little window and saw the driver of his wagon pull up the horses to a standstill and jump down to join the troubled crew, wherever the wagon was down. Cotton pulled on his breeches and a shirt and dashed, barefoot, out into the cold rain. Sure enough, a wagon was tilted precariously over the edge of the road, dangerously close to falling into a ditch. Only the tugging and pulling of the men kept it from falling into the raging, muddy water.

Six or seven of them were thigh-deep in the ditch, supporting the side of the wagon so that it wouldn't go over. After two hours of struggle and the hard, back-breaking work of the men and the horses, the wagon was back on the road, ready to go again.

The tired, sleepy crew would work the circus the next day. The kinkers, soaked to the skin, crept back to their wagons for a few last winks of sleep before time to make a proper entrance into town.

"Wake up, Cotton," Al's voice called as he beat on the wagon door. "It's dawn and we have to roll into town looking bright and shiny. It's our last stop of the season, remember? And your big day!"

Cotton rolled over and burrowed his head into the down pillow. He was barely conscious that the wagons had stopped moving. Then he sat upright, his sleepiness thrown aside like an old coat he had outgrown and didn't need anymore.

Today was his big day! The day he would perform with the Bailey Circus for the very first time. His moment to prove his worth to all of them, to Ma, to Aunt Mollie, to Al, to Birda, to Leo and Nino. Most of all, to Lotta.

Cotton jumped out of bed and climbed into dry clothes. He put on a long, red coat with brass buttons, his storm parade coat. When the circus entered a town in the rain, there was no point in ruining their regular costumes in the parade. They all wore the long coats over their clothes. If anyone was brave enough to be waiting for them in the pre-dawn rain, the kinkers would look like real performers, not the bedraggled, soaked group they really were.

Cotton could hear the band strike up, playing "Dixie," and he knew that somewhere ahead, leading them all, was Aunt Mollie, dressed in her usual finery, heedless of the rain.

"You have to give the folks what they came to see," she always said. "Look happy and glad to be here. They'll pick it up and cheer you on."

It always worked. For some reason, rainy-day shows were always received with the most applause, the most enthusiastic cheering. Maybe it was just to spite the weather that had tried to spoil their fun!

Getting the circus tents up in the heavy rain was another challenge for the crew, but they seemed to welcome the change from ordinary routine. Everything was ready for the folks' enjoyment, right on schedule.

As soon as the last bleacher was in place, the Flying Morenos started putting up their rigging. Each connection had to be checked and double-checked; each rope of the web had to hang just right. The Morenos owned their own rigging and would allow no one else to touch it. Their lives depended on its being put together perfectly.

"Ready to go!" Papa Moreno yelled. Leo nodded, satisfied.

"D'ya want to give it one last turn, Cotton?" Leo asked. "Make sure we've got the time just right?"

"Yes," Cotton answered, his throat dry. "I'd better. I'll change and be right with you."

An hour later, Cotton left the big top, grinning in self-satisfaction. He could do it blindfolded. Humming, he fed Bolivar and ran to the mess tent for breakfast before the big parade.

He was finishing off the last of his grits and eggs with the help of one of Fred the cook's famous biscuits when Aunt Mollie and Birda came in and sat down with him.

"My, you look happy this morning, Cotton," Aunt Mollie said. "Are you ready for your big day?"

"Yes'm," Cotton managed to get out around his last mouthful of grits.

"I know you'll be wonderful, Cotton," Birda said softly. "I watched you, and you seem to belong up there."

"Gol, Birda, thanks." Cotton didn't know what to say to this shy little girl who looked at him with so much faith and admiration. He was so embarrassed, he jumped up from the table and left, not looking back.

The parade was short and rain-soaked. Birda did not ride atop Bolivar; Nino took her place. Cotton, hunched into his coat, rode on the roof of the bandwagon. Aunt Mollie had decided not to extend it to its full height in the rain.

With the parade over, the circus people relaxed for an hour before dressing for the afternoon performance. Cotton was too excited to rest. He paced up and down the menagerie tent, listening to Bolivar snort and occasionally trumpet, lifting his trunk high in the air.

Soon it was time for Cotton to change into his fancy new white tights and spangles. He wondered what his ma would say if she knew what her youngest son was doing today. Most likely, she'd just give him one brief thought, then go on with her ironing.

Well, when he was famous, she'd have to be proud of him. He would buy her a fine new dress and hat and bring her to the circus to watch him perform. Her eyes would light up when she saw him up there in the air, flying like a bird. And Joe and Will would be speechless, seeing his act. Annie would squeal with delight, and he'd see that she had all the cotton candy and peanuts she could eat.

Cotton's daydreams ended a few minutes before the Grand Parade, the tournament, was due to start. He put on shoes and cape and ran to the kinkers' entrance by the bandstand. The band struck up a lively tune as the ring-master, Al, shouted into his megaphone.

"Ladies and gentlemen . . . and children of all ages!"

The crowd hushed and listened for the announcement.

"Today we are pleased to present to you an all new Mollie Bailey Show. A Texas show for Texas people!"

The crowd roared its approval.

"And now, let's give a big welcome to our performers and trained animals as they pass before your eyes in our Grand Entrance Parade!"

The cornet player sent a flourish of golden, brassy notes into the air, and the band struck up a march.

Leading the parade was Bolivar, this time with Birda, dressed in an Eastern costume of filmy harem pants and jingling coin jewelry, riding in a *howdah* on his back. Her golden hair tossed in the light as she turned from side to side, waving at the crowd.

The clowns followed, cavorting and jousting with each other. Shetland ponies, dogs and ring horses; acrobats and jugglers and balancing acts. From a special wagon, carved with golden dragons breathing golden fire, the Flying Morenos waved to the cheering crowd. Cotton's heart stopped when he saw Lotta in a scant costume of some filmy red material, her black hair covered in a purple turban. She carried a huge fan of white ostrich feathers and waved it back and forth as she passed by the shouting audience. She was beautiful.

Then followed cages with the wild animals: monkeys, coyote, cheetah, and a wild boar. Then came the zebras, Zondra and Zandie, and the camel, El Mar.

Cotton knew them all now. How different he felt about the circus than he had a few months ago. He was part of it now, part of all these people and the animals and the band and the roustabouts. And Aunt Mollie, most of all. He felt he had never belonged to anyone before in his whole life, the way he belonged to Aunt Mollie and the circus.

After the camel and zebras had brought up the rear of the Grand Parade, Cotton went backstage to wait for his cue.

He saw Lotta heading for her dressing area behind the bandstand. He wanted to tell her how beautiful she looked, but he was afraid she'd laugh at him. So he stood, watching her and wishing she'd speak to him.

She did.

"Well, Cotton, are you ready for your big day?" she said with a smile that sent Cotton's heart reeling.

"I guess so, Lotta," was all he could get out of his parched throat.

"Don't let the demon in, that's all, and you'll be fine." With that she turned and walked away from him, leaving Cotton bewildered and troubled.

Demon? What demon? What did she mean?

Leo came sauntering up at that moment and Cotton blurted out, "Lotta told me not to let the 'demon' in. What did she mean, Leo?"

"Oh, that Lotta. She should have her mouth washed out with a bar of lye soap! Pay no attention to her. Just do your act like we've been doing it. Everything will be fine, I promise you, boy."

Leo left as suddenly as he had appeared. Well, he said not to worry, so Cotton decided he wouldn't worry. Everything would be fine.

Wouldn't it?

65

11

The Demon Whispers

Backstage, Cotton followed the progress of the circus by the music. He knew which piece was the background for Bolivar and Birda; which for the clowns; which for Allie's slack wire act.

He waited for only one sound, the trumpet blare which heralded the Flying Morenos into the arena. When he heard it, after what seemed like a lifetime, he jumped up and followed the Moreno family as they ran, waving, to the center of the ring. Cotton ran too, waving at the cheering crowd and hopping over the dirt ring, careful to put his right foot first. He stayed a little behind the Morenos as they took their bows, flourishing capes and throwing kisses to the audience.

Lotta was first with her act on the rings. When she started the one-arm plange, the crowd hushed in awe of the small body being thrown over and over itself. Then they took up the count: twenty-one, twenty-two, twenty-three. They chanted the numbers and, when Lotta slowed her rotation and waved from above that she was finished, they had counted up to fifty-eight. Someday she would go to one hundred and beyond, she had told Leo one day while Cotton had stood by, spellbound.

Today he joined the audience in applause for the talent and beauty that was Lotta.

Then Leo and Nino did their flying act, with double somersaults to their father and triple pirouettes on the return. As always, the crowd loved them and cheered and clapped for each trick.

It was here. The time for Cotton to perform for the first time ever, before an audience!

With confidence, he walked over to the web and began his climb to the platform where Nino waited. Leo was already seated on the catchbar, lazily swinging back and forth.

"Ladies and gentlemen! May I have your attention!" Al shouted in his best ringmaster voice.

"Today we have, for the very first time, a young performer who will thrill you with his work. He is none other than . . ."

The cornet sounded a three-note blast.

" . . . Cotton Bailey. Folks, I give you the youngest aerialist with the Bailey Show. Give him a big hand . . . Cotton Bailey!"

Cotton had reached the platform just in time to turn and wave and smile at the crowd. He wiped his hands on the resin bag and nodded to Leo, who went into his leglock.

Nino handed Cotton the flybar. Leo started his backswing.

The drum rolled, cymbals clashed. The audience was completely still.

Cotton leaped into the air, holding the flybar with both hands, swinging his body back and forth, upward and back, gaining speed.

On his second swing out, Cotton heard Leo call, "Break." He released the bar and started the backward somersault.

Time slowed. He was barely moving. His mind traveled to places he had never seen before, then, like a pendulum, swung back to the present.

What was happening? He should have connected with Leo's firm hands by now. But no, he was still sailing, slowly, slowly through the air.

A small voice spoke to him.

"Why do you try so hard, Cotton? Wouldn't it be easier for you to let go?"

Like an echo in his ears, it repeated, over and over, "Let go. Let go. Let go."

He had to get rid of the voice. Maybe if he closed his eyes a moment. As though in a nightmare, he floated above his body hurtling through the air. Watching, he saw himself flatten out and start to fall.

"COTTON!"

It was Leo's voice. But, too late, he was falling through the air, falling, falling. . . .

He hit the net and bounced, then landed on his feet and did a rollover off the edge.

The crowd gave a quick gasp and started to applaud, uncertainly at first, then gaining in volume. Perhaps they thought this was part of the act, he thought miserably. Well, they wouldn't think so when they saw him run out of the top in disgrace.

Forever in disgrace.

He heard the band pick up the music for the Morenos and knew that the show was continuing without him.

Forever without him.

Tears streamed down his cheeks. What had happened to him? Why had he been such a coward? Such a failure?

He ran to the menagerie tent and threw himself down on the straw beside Bolivar. He should have stuck to elephant feeding, he thought, should have known he couldn't do anything better. What would Aunt Mollie think of him now?

And Lotta . . . oh, gol.

He pulled his knees up under his chin and wrapped

his arms around his legs. With his head on his knees he sobbed and sobbed until the sobs were dry rasps and he had no more tears.

When he heard the music which signaled the end of the circus, he knew he had to get out of there. He couldn't face anyone. Mostly he couldn't bear to face Lotta.

As he turned to go, Bolivar gave a snort. The bull was hungry. Cotton would give him a few forks full of hay, for the last time, and then leave.

And never, never come back.

Before he could finish with Bolivar, he saw Birda come rushing toward him. She was crying.

"Oh, Cotton, I know how you feel. But you mustn't give up."

Cotton could only shake his head and say, "No! No!"

"Yes, Cotton, you must go back up and go on with your work. You're really talented, you know. Don't give it up, please."

He turned away from Birda. It hurt too much to listen to her encouraging him to go back. He knew where he belonged. Where he should never have left — with Ma and Joe and Will and little Annie. Not here. Not in the circus.

"Don't try to convince him, Birda. He knows what happened, don't you, Cotton?" It was Lotta's voice, and there was a strange note of triumph in it. She had never wanted him to succeed. She was glad he had fallen.

Birda looked at Lotta for a moment and then turned and left the menagerie.

"Some people just aren't cut out to be aerialists, Cotton," Lotta went on. "I guess you're one of them. Nice try, though. Maybe you could try juggling." She tossed her black hair and left Cotton alone.

With an effort he rose and ran as fast as his numb legs could carry him to where the bandwagon sat, waiting for the musicians to pack away their instruments for the night.

He ran inside and slammed the door. Then he peeled

off his costume and carefully folded it, placing it on his bed. Someone else could wear it. Someone who wouldn't always fail. After putting on his clothes, he pushed the rest of his belongings into the old pillowcase he had brought with him.

He had to hurry. He couldn't face Aunt Mollie. She must be so disappointed in him.

Cotton let himself out of the wagon and looked around. People were streaming out of the big top. The circus was over. Aunt Mollie would be standing at the entrance saying goodbye to folks, "Come back, next time, y'hear?"

He ran around the back end of the wagon and struck out across the field. Maybe he could get away without being seen.

The town they were in, Bellville, was west of Huntsville, so he tried to figure which way east would be. The sun had never shown its face that day, although the rain had stopped. He was thankful for that.

He would walk till dark, then find a barn or some shelter to sleep in. About dawn, if he was lucky, he might get a ride with a farmer going to market.

Somehow, he'd make it home to Ma.

It was sunset of the second day when Cotton finally saw the outskirts of Huntsville before him. A sudden wave of homesickness swept over him. Would Ma be glad to see him? He couldn't wait to see little Annie. He started to run.

A dim light came from the kitchen as he finally approached the house. His chest burned like fire from running so fast, but he couldn't slow down.

He burst into the house.

"Ma! I'm home!"

It was as if he'd never been away. His mother stood at the woodstove, stirring something in her big soup kettle. She glanced up at him and ran her hand through her thin hair.

71

"Jeremiah? That you? Wash up, it's near time for supper."

No greeting. No questions. Didn't she want to know how he'd done all those months? Didn't she care?

Cotton — Jeremiah — went to the sink and pumped out enough water to wet his hands. He dried them on the towel hanging on a hook beside the pump.

"Where's everybody, Ma? Where's Annie?"

"Joe and Will are out workin', tryin' to make a little money so's we can make ends meet," his mother said, her voice toneless. "How comes you come home, Jeremiah? Does that mean you lost your job, you won't be sendin' money anymore?"

Was that all he meant to her?

"Where's Annie, Ma?" He wouldn't put an answer to her question.

"I sent her upstairs with no supper. She sassed me."

"But, Ma, she's only four years old. She doesn't know any better."

"Well, I reckon she'll learn, won't she?"

Jeremiah looked at his mother, as though for the first time. He thought of Aunt Mollie, of her kindness and how she always thought the best of folks. Ma probably couldn't help it, but she wasn't kind. She always thought people were naturally bad and that you had to keep tight control over them, or they'd get "outa hand."

He wanted to cry, for his mother, for his family, for himself. Instead he climbed the stairs and called to Annie.

When she heard his voice she came running.

"Jeremiah! You're back! Oh, goody, you're home!"

At least one member of the family was glad to see him. He had to be thankful for that.

12

Aunt Mollie's Invitation

Life had settled back to the ordinary run of things for Jeremiah. Two weeks had gone by. He still had dreams at night of the voice in his head and of falling and being disgraced. Sometimes he dreamed of Birda. She was far away and calling to him. He wanted to go, but something held him back.

He never dreamed of Lotta.

During the day he kept busy, entertaining Annie and fetching and carrying for Ma.

Today was wash day, so he was lugging hot water from the stove to the backyard, where Ma was slicing lye soap into a big metal tub. He had been heating water on the stove and carrying it out to the tub since right after daybreak. In all that time Ma hadn't said one word to him. He guessed she was mad about the loss of his three dollars a week.

"Ho, out there! Anybody home?"

Aunt Mollie! He'd know her voice anywhere! He had to hide. He couldn't face her after his disgrace, his failure.

"There you are, Cotton," Aunt Mollie said, giving

73

him a big hug. "Tarnation, you gave us a turn. Couldn't figure where you'd gone for a day or two. Then I had to see to closin' up the show for the winter and gettin' all the kinkers off. It was a wild west show, just about! Anyway, I finally had a moment to catch my breath, and I said to Gus, "Why, Cotton's gone home to Huntsville that's where he's gone! And, sure enough, here you are."

Aunt Mollie looked toward Jeremiah's mother. "Mornin', Mrs. Colquitt. How've you been?"

"Fair to middlin', Miz Bailey. Have you come to give Jeremiah his job back?"

"Ma!" Cotton felt the flush start at the back of his neck and race all the way to his scalp.

"Well, actually, Mrs. Colquitt, I did come to ask Cotton if he'd be so kind as to return to the circus. We miss him and need him there."

"I'm sure he'll take kindly to that notion, won't you, Jeremiah?"

He didn't know what to say. He wanted to believe Aunt Mollie, that they needed and wanted him back. Gol, how he wished he could believe that.

"Uh, Aunt Mollie, I don't know. I let you and Leo and Nino down. I spoiled their act. I don't know how it happened, but this voice kept saying, 'Let go, let go' so I did and then I was falling onto the net. I'm so sorry I disgraced you. . . ."

He could no longer stop the tears which had been waiting behind his eyes for release. Sobbing, he ran to Aunt Mollie, who gathered him into her arms and sang little soft words into his ear.

"Come back with me, Cotton. You didn't disgrace anyone. Tarnation, sounds to me like the demon got to you."

"Demon?" Cotton asked, his eyes wide, remembering Lotta's words.

"That's what the kinkers call it. It's a voice inside the aerialist's head, urgin' him to 'let go,' as you said. For some reason they call it 'castin'.' Don't know why. I've known many a good performer listen to the voice. Some were killed. You were lucky we had the net beneath you.

"Don't you worry a minute about it, son. Just shows you're one of us, a real trouper! And now you know about the demon, you can close your ears to him anytime he comes around. He'll get tired of tryin' and give up on you."

"Do you really mean it, Aunt Mollie? I could try again?"

"You have the makin's of a very fine aerialist, Cotton, but you're also a very fine student. I'd like to see you go to college someday and make somethin' of yourself. Circus is fine for us circus folks who've been at it forever, but you can have another future, a better one, if you want.

"I been holdin' two dollars a week out of your pay, savin' it for your schoolin'. If you come back, I'll keep savin' for you and, between us, we'll have enough for college by the time you're old enough. What do you say?"

"Is it all right with you, Ma? If I go back with Aunt Mollie and stay with the circus?"

"You'll send me the three dollars ever' week, like you been doin'?"

"Yes, Ma."

"Then I can't see no reason for you to stay here. Go pack your things and I'll give Miz Bailey a cup of tea."

It took two minutes to pack his few things in the pillowcase. He hugged Annie.

"I love you, Annie," he said, kissing the little girl on the cheek.

"I love you too, Jeremiah," Annie said.

His goodbyes said, Jeremiah followed Aunt Mollie out to her little black cart. He patted Mariah on the neck and climbed in beside Aunt Mollie, who sat straight and proud and said, "Giddap, Mariah," in a soft voice.

The horse started down the road. Cotton looked back to see Annie waving. His ma was not in sight. Someday he'd go back and make it easier for his ma. And he'd see that Annie had everything she could ever want. When he was out of college and a doctor. Yep, a doctor was what he'd be.

But until then, wasn't it wonderful that he could spend his days and nights with the Mollie Bailey Show, feeding Bolivar and — maybe, just maybe — being a flyer again?

He couldn't wait to see Birda to tell her his plans for the future.

Gol. It was good to be Cotton Bailey again.

Afterword

There really was a "Cotton Bailey," although his participation in the circus as well as the time frame were fictionalized by the author. His name was Serge T. Urling, and he joined the Bailey circus when he was ten, remaining until he was eighteen. Aunt Mollie renamed him "Cotton Bailey." He later became a doctor.

Aunt Mollie's husband, Gus Bailey, died in Houston, Texas, in 1896. At that time the circus was at its peak size: thirty-one wagons, one hundred seventy head of stock, twenty-one trained ponies and other "led" stock, or walking animals. The payroll numbered some sixty employees.

In October 1906, Aunt Mollie converted the Mollie Bailey Circus to a railroad show, with three special cars: one Pullman and two freight cars. The Pullman was fitted with staterooms, dining room, and kitchen. This would be her home on the road for the rest of her days. By 1913 she had added eight flatcars, two stock cars, and a thirty-day advance car.

Each stop along the road meant open house in Mollie's car. Many well-known Texans, including Texas Governor James Stephen Hogg, enjoyed her hospitality.

Another acquaintance was Comanche chief Quanah Parker, son of white captive Cynthia Ann Parker. Each time the circus played Quanah, Texas, where the old chief often visited, he asked Mollie to recount the episode of the Indian raid and how she scared off the braves by beating on the big circus drum. He is said to have laughed and laughed at the story and never tired of hearing it.

Mollie Bailey introduced the first movies to Texas, showing them in a sideshow tent.

In her later years, Mollie Bailey remarried. Her husband, much younger than she, was A. H. (Blackie) Hardesty. According to one story, she married him because he was a good "chandelier man," who tended to the lighting for the circus. "Shandy men" were hard to find and harder to keep. She supposedly also renamed him Blackie Bailey, and said she would be called Mrs. Blackie Bailey.

When her daughter Birda fell ill, Mollie left the circus and took her to Houston. Birda died in 1917, leaving a husband, Charles C. Dickens, and three children. The heart went out of Aunt Mollie then. In the autumn of 1918 she fell in her yard and died on October 2, 1918.

Her sons tried to run the circus without her, but it was unsuccessful. Mollie had never given them enough authority to learn the business, and, without her to lead them, they soon gave up. For a couple of years, until the mid-1920s, they ran a moving picture show out of a truck and traveled throughout Louisiana and Mississippi.

The Mollie A. Bailey Show was no more, but for many years afterward people remembered attending her circus. It was often the only entertainment they ever had as children, besides "spellin' bees and barn warmin's."

She was rightly called the "Circus Queen of the Southwest."

Glossary of Circus Terms

ACROBAT: Performer who does tricks with his body.

AERIALIST: Person who performs in the top of the circus tent, swinging on the trapeze and "flying" through the air to another aerialist (see Flyer and Catcher).

BIG TOP: Main tent.

BLEACHERS: Rows of backless seats made of wooden boards supported by posts, and usually (in the circus) painted blue (see Blues).

BLOWDOWN: When circus tent is knocked down by storm.

BLUES: Nickname for bleachers.

BULL: Elephant.

BULL MAN: Keeper of the elephant.

CANDY BUTCHER: Man who sells candy.

CASTING: Term used by aerialists for the voice in their heads that says, "Let go, let go!".

CATCHER: Aerialist who swings on the trapeze by his knees and catches hold of his partner, who is flying free of his own trapeze.

CLEM: Circus name for a fight.

EQUESTRIENNE: Woman who does fancy horseback riding.

FLYBAR: Trapeze bar used by the flyer.

FLYER: Aerialist who leaves the trapeze and "flies" into the hands of his partner, swinging from another trapeze.

GRIFTER: Crook.

HAY THE BULL: Feed the elephant.

"HEY, RUBE":   Circus man's call for help when a fight starts.

HOWDAH: Platform on elephant's back where performer rides.

JOEY: Clown, named after Joe Grimaldi, early clown.

JUGGLER: Performer who tosses and catches several objects in the air at the same time.

KINKER: Performer.

LAYOUT: Simple trick on trapeze.

MECHANIC: Wide leather band worn around waist, with ropes attached to pulley. Worn by circus performers to prevent falls when practicing dangerous or difficult acts.

MENAGERIE: Tent where circus animals are kept.

ONE-ARMED PLANGE: Trick where the aerialist throws her body over and over itself, while hanging by one arm.

PAPER THE TOWN: Put circus posters up in towns where the circus will be showing soon.

PATTER: Coach.

PIKE POSITION: An aerialist's stance in the air, where the legs are held out in front to right angle of the body, toes pointed.

PIROUETTE: Twisting turn done in midair by aerialist.

RIGGING: Equipment the aerialist uses in his act.

RINGMASTER: Announcer for the circus.

ROUGHNECKS: Men who do the heavy work on the circus.

SLACK WIRE: Loosely strung wire, on which performer walks.

SUNDAY SCHOOL: A circus term meaning clean and honest.

TANBARK: The bark of oak, used on floors of indoor arenas.

TOP: Tent.

TOURNAMENT: Grand parade at the start of the circus.

TRAP: Trapeze.

WEB: Series of ropes in the aerialist's rigging.

Bibliography

Abernethy, Francis E., ed. *Legendary Ladies of Texas.* "Mollie Bailey," by Martha Hartzog. Dallas: E-Heart Press, 1981.

American Heritage. *Great Days of the Circus.* New York: 1962.

Andrew, Matthew Page, comp. *Women of the South in War Times.* The Norman, Remington Co., 1920.

Bailey, Olga. *Mollie Bailey: The Circus Queen of the Southwest.* Dallas: Harben-Spotts Co., Inc., 1943.

Burrow, George. *Romano Lavo-Lil, A Book of the Gypsy.* Gloucester: Alan Sutton, 1982.

Campbell, R. Wright. *Circus Couronne.* New York: Simon & Schuster, 1977.

Carmer, Carl. *Stars Fell on Alabama.* New York: Farrar & Rinehart, Inc., 1934.

Conklin, George, with Harvey W. Root. *The Ways of the Circus.* New York: Harper Bros., no date.

Country Beautiful Magazine. *Circus!* Wisconsin: State Historical Society, 1964.

Croft-Cooke, Rupert, and Peter Cotes. *Circus — A World History.* New York: Macmillan Pub., 1976.

Cros, Helen Reeder. *The Real Tom Thumb.* New York: Four Winds Press, 1980.

Duncan, Thomas W. *Gus, the Great.* New York: Lippincott Co., 1947.

Durant, John, and Alice Durant. *Pictorial History of the American Circus.* A. S. Barnes, Inc., 1957.

Fenner, M. S., and W. Fenner. *The Circus: Lure and Legend.* New York: Prentice-Hall, 1970.

Fox, Charles Phillip, and Tom Parkinson. *The Circus in America.* Waukesha, WI: Country Beautiful, 1969.

Gaona, T., with Harry L. Graham. *Born to Fly.* Los Angeles: Wild Rose, 1984.

Gollman, Robert H. *My Father Owned a Circus.* Idaho: Coxton Printers, 1965.

Hamilton, Sgt. D. H. *History of Company M — First Texas Volunteer Infantry, Hood's Brigade.* Waco, TX: W. M. Morrison, 1962.

81

Hawks, Clarence. *Dapples of the Circus.* New York: Platt & Munk Co, Inc., 1943.

Holt, R. D. "The Old Gray Mare." *Cattleman,* September 1953.

Houston Public Library. *Scrapbook.*

Hunter, J. Marvin, Sr. "Mollie Bailey, Great Showwoman." *Frontier Times* 27, No. 7, April 1950.

Jaenecke, Chylene. "Mollie Bailey." *Junior Historian.* Austin: Texas State Historical Association, September-May, 1959–1961.

Jones, Edgar R. *Those Were the Good Old Days.* New York: Simon & Schuster, 1979.

Jones, Katharine M., ed. *Heroines of Dixie: Spring of High Hopes.* New York: Bobbs-Merrill Co., Inc., 1955.

Kane, Harnett T. *Natchez on the Mississippi.* New York: Wm. Morrow & Co., 1947.

———. *A Picture Story of the Confederacy.* New York: Lothrop, Lee & Shepard Co., Inc., 1965.

King, Edward. *Texas: 1874.* Houston: Cordovan Press, 1974.

Knox, Rose B. *Footlights Afloat.* New York: Doubleday, 1937.

Lasswell, Mary, ed. *Rags and Hope, the Recollections of Val C. Giles, Four Years with Hood's Brigade, Fourth Texas Infantry, 1861–1865.* New York: Coward-McCann, Inc., 1961.

Laver, James. *Costume and Fashion.* London: Thames & Hudson, Ltd., 1969 and 1982.

Levenson, Dorothy. *The First Book of the Confederacy.* New York: Franklin Watts, 1968.

———. *The First Book of the Civil War.* New York: Franklin Watts, 1977.

Maguire, Jack. "Mollie Bailey's Circus Show." *Southwest Airlines Magazine* 9, No. 1, June 1979.

Mankowitz, Wolf. *Mazeppa.* Dublin: Imeartas Ltd., 1982.

Mitchell, Lebbeus. *The Circus Comes to Town.* New York: Cupples & Leon, 1921.

Monroe, Marshall. "Memories Are Recalled of Mollie Bailey." *Houston Chronicle,* October 27, 1929.

Norwood, Edwin P. *The Circus Menagerie.* Junior Literary Guild: 1929.

Nunn, Joan. *Fashion in Costume, 1200–1980.* New York: Schocken Books, 1984.

Patteson, Ikie Gray. *Loose Leaves: a History of Delta County.* Dallas: Mathis Pub. Co., 1935.

Pember, Phoebe Yates. *A Southern Woman's Story.* New York: McCowat-Mercer Press, Inc., 1959.

Petry, Ann. *Harriet Tubman, Conductor on the Underground Railroad.* New York: Pocket Books, 1955.

Phares, Ros. "Mollie Bailey, Circus Queen." *Texas Parade,* March 1952.

Polley, J. B. *A Soldier's Letters to Charming Nellie.* New York: Neale Pub., 1908.

Rickard, J. A. *Brief Biographies of Brave Texans.* Dallas: Hendrick-Long Pub. Co., 1962.

Schaffner, N. E., with V. Johnson. *The Fabulous Toby & Me.* New York: Prentice-Hall, 1968.

Seago, Edward. *Circus Company — Life on the Road with the Travelling Show.* London: Putnam, 1933.

Simpson, Harold B. *Hood's Texas Brigade.* Waco, TX: Texian Press, 1970.

———. "Mollie Bailey, The Circus Queen of the Southwest." Collection. *Women of Texas.* Waco, TX: Texian Press, 1972.

Slout, William Lawrence. *Theatre in a Tent.* Bowling Green, KY: 1972.

Syers, William Edward. *Off the Beaten Trail.* 1963.

Tarkington, Booth. *The Gentleman from Indiana.* New York: Grosset & Dunlap, 1902.

Texas Mothers' Committee. *Worthy Mothers of Texas: 1776–1976.* Belton, TX: Stillhouse Hollow Pub., 1976.

Tolbert, Frank X. "Aunt Mollie and Circus Lots." *Dallas News,* November 8, 1959.

Watkins, T. H. *Mark Twain's Mississippi.* Palo Alto, CA: American West Pub. Co., 1974.

Wayman, Norbury L. *Life on the River.* New York: Crown Pub., 1971.

Webb, Walter P., ed. *The Handbook of Texas, Vol I.* Austin: Texas State Historical Association, 1952.

Winkler, Mrs. A. V. *The Confederate Capital and Hood's Texas Brigade.* Austin: Eugene Von Boeckmann, 1894.

Worrell, Estelle Ansley. *Children's Costume in America, 1607–1910.* New York: Charles Scribner's Sons, 1980.

Writer's Program of WPA. *Mississippi: A Guide to the Magnolia State.* New York: Hastings House, 1938.

———. *Alabama: A Guide to the State.* New York: Hastings House, 1941.

———. *Arkansas: A Guide to the State.* New York: Hastings House, 1941.